Happiness Awaits You!

68 true stories
44 authors

Written and Compiled By
Ca rol Costa
Liisa Kyle
Maggie TerryViale

Open Books
PRESS

Published by Open Books Press, USA
www.openbookspress.com

An imprint of Pen & Publish, Inc.
Bloomington, Indiana
(812) 837-9226
info@PenandPublish.com

www.PenandPublish.com

Cover acrylic on paper painting Allowing Joy
by and courtesy of Maggie TerrryViale

ISBN: 978-0-9844600-5-2

This book is printed on acid free paper.

Printed in the USA

Happiness Awaits You!

Everyone wants to be happy, but not everyone knows how to be happy. People often seek happiness in personal relationships, careers, and material possessions, not realizing that true happiness comes from within. This book will show readers how to nurture their inner joy and share it with others. It will show them how to handle the challenges of life with humor and courage. They will learn to trust their own instincts and allow themselves to be happy and content.

The three co-authors bring a combination of expertise and metaphysical experience to this book that results in a blending of inspirational true stories and expert advice that will help readers cope with everyday problems.

Each chapter focuses on specific issues encountered in relationships, work and personal growth and will encourage readers to become stronger in faith and hope. This includes segments called "Stepping Stones" relating to the theme of each chapter. Stepping Stones are practical guidelines that will reinforce the underlying purpose of the book that is to bring readers to a place in their lives where doubt and uncertainty are no longer a roadblock to happiness.

About the Authors

Carol Costa is a professional writer and editor. She is also an award-winning playwright and a journalist. Carol has worked as an editor of books and newspapers, a business news correspondent, and managed a literary agency. Carol's plays have been published and produced in New York City, Los Angeles, and regional theaters across the country. Her published books include: *Ask Aunt Emma* and *Invisible Force*, paranormal mysteries, Champagne Books, *The Master Plan* and *A Deadly Hand*, mystery series, *Love Steals the Scene* and *Labor of Love*, romance novels, Avalon Books, *Teach Yourself Accounting in 24 Hours*, (1st & 2nd Editions) , *The Complete Idiot's Guide to Surviving Bankruptcy, Teach Yourself Bookkeeping in 24 Hours* and *The Complete Idiot's Guide to Starting and Running a Thrift Store*, Penguin USA, *Video Poker: Play Longer with Less Risk*, ECW Press. Visit her website at: www.carolcostaauthor.com.

Liisa Kyle is an internationally published writer/editor/photographer. She earned her Ph.D. in Psychology from the University of Michigan. As an international consultant, she has coached individuals, facilitated groups, and delivered inventive workshops on four continents. Dr. Kyle specializes in coaching creative people (www.liisakyle.com) and providing solutions for multi-talented people (www.davincidilemma.com). Her personal artistic pursuits include working in metal, glass, clay, textiles, paper and more. Her creative works have been featured in galleries, art fairs and juried exhibitions. She has volunteered as an adult literacy tutor and has fostered and trained Guide Dog puppies for the Blind.

Maggie TerryViale has been an artist for over twenty years, showing her paintings at galleries and museums on both coasts. She has studied art at UC Davis and earned a Master of Fine Arts Degree from the San Francisco Art Institute. Her awards in this field include two grants from the Pollack-Krasner Foundation. Maggie is also a writer who has studied at UCLA extension Master's Class and taken workshops at The Maui Writing Conference, The Screenwriting Conference at Santa Fe and at Pima Community College in Arizona. Her scripts have won awards in contests such as Fade In, The Maui Screenwriting Contest, and the Austin Film Festival Contest. She's also a healer, a Third Degree Reiki Master and a Reverend. Following Guidance she wishes to be of service to others on their path. Visit her website at: www.HopeHealingHands.com.

TABLE OF CONTENTS

CHAPTER 4 Joy in the Workplace

Most people spend the majority of their time at work. Stories in this chapter demonstrate how to find joy from 9 to 5 and how to accept and respect co-workers.

Stepping Stones: Advice on choosing the career that will make you happy, as well as advice on how to enjoy your work even if it is not your ideal job.

CHAPTER 5 Was It Only a Dream?

Messages received in dreams can be prophetic or simply a reflection of the subconscious thoughts that rise to the surface during the sleep process. Stories of dreams that came true and how dream images can guide you on your path to joy.

Stepping Stones: Advice on how to analyze your dreams and how to put yourself in a good frame of mind before falling asleep so that your dreams will be beneficial.

CHAPTER 6 Blessings in Disguise

Stories about weathering the storms of change and learning that the disappointments and setbacks that trouble us are often a detour that leads us to the path we are meant to follow.

Stepping Stones: Advice on how to face adversity with a positive attitude.

CHAPTER 7 Have I Lived Before?

Reincarnation is a mystery that must be considered and either accepted or rejected by each individual person. Unusual stories from people who believe they have lived before and brought their experiences and knowledge into their current lives.

Stepping Stones: Advice on how to remember past lives and solve problems through meditation or past lives therapy.

CHAPTER 8 Are We There Yet

This chapter is about the tools that can help us know ourselves better so that we can grow spiritually. Stories about meditation and messages from their higher selves, angels and spirit guides.
Stepping Stones: Information on how to meditate including suggestions for opening yourself up to the wisdom and knowledge you are meant to receive to help you on your life's journey.

CHAPTER 9 Acceptance

This chapter will be especially helpful to people who are frustrated when they feel they are losing control of things in their lives. Stories about accepting and learning from events you don't want to experience.
Stepping Stones: Simple advice on how to accept the things you cannot control in your life.

CHAPTER 10 Recovering From Loss
We all suffer losses and must learn to handle the emotions

that accompany them. Stories about dealing with grief and messages from the other side may help readers find the strength and determination to move on with their lives.

Stepping Stones: Advice on how to cope with trauma and loss.

CHAPTER 11 The Power of Forgiveness   231
Holding onto anger, hate and bitterness is destructive. Stories about forgiveness and its healing power.

Stepping Stones: Advice on how to forgive yourself and others.

CHAPTER 12 The Circle of Life   257
A ring is round and has no end, so the circle of life continues. Stories about near-death experiences and communicating with the spirit world.

Stepping Stones: Examining your feelings about life after death.

CHAPTER 1
Minor Miracles

Sometimes we think things are impossible. Sometimes we give up hope completely. Sometimes we fall into the crevices of life that are deep, dark shadows. We curl up, expecting the worse and our chattering mind doesn't seem to be still. How do we find the courage to continue? Do we sit around waiting, hoping, praying for a miracle? Or is there something we can do ourselves? Yes, miracles can and do happen, but if they don't, then what? Are there minor miracles that we can allow? Can we shift our attitude on a dime? If so, how?

On a cloudy day in Los Angeles an artist was feeling lost and alone. Everything seemed bleak, and no matter what she did nothing was going right. She was frustrated with the way the painting she was working on was turning into a boring, brown ball of nothingness. She moped around the house in a total funk until finally she had enough. She went outside and sat on the cold cement steps with her head lowered down. It was then that she saw it.

Peeking out from the weeds, a single crimson nasturtium bloomed. Its soft velvet petals drizzled with dew, splashing rainbow sparkles all around. The artist stared at God's creation, perfect and majestic in every way. The vibrant color energized her being with a richness that was unexplainable. She savored its glory and it nourished her soul. Time seemed to stand still as she drank in its beauty. It might have been seconds, it could have been fifteen minutes, but when she rose to go back into the house, she knew a minor miracle had occurred. A four-petalled flower had revived her soul.

Look for these miracles in your life. They could be as simple as a child giggling in a grocery store, or sighting a pair of hummingbirds dancing in a nearby tree, or clouds that you'd swear looked like wispy white angel wings drifting in the azure sky. And while we're talking about miracles, don't be afraid to be a miracle worker yourself. Smile at someone who needs a ray of hope; say a kind word to someone who needs it most. Pick a daisy and give it to a homeless stranger.

Yes, daily, miracles occur, the sun comes out shinning and we are hopeful once again. In this chapter we will examine stories that give us hope, encourage us to move ahead, and to trust there is a new day dawning for all of us.

Angel Wings
By Carol Costa

Do you believe in angels? More specifically do you believe in guardian angels? When I was a little girl, I was taught that everyone on earth has a special angel that watches over them. Now I believe that angels take many forms and don't necessarily have the wings and halos depicted in pictures. I believe that some angels are living breathing humans just like us. They come in and out of our lives bringing us love, laughter, kind words, or lessons we must learn in this lifetime. These people represent minor miracles that we often don't even notice. However, this story is not about an angel encased in a body that you can see. It is about an angel, or maybe in this case a squadron of angels, that came to my aid one hot summer day.

It was my youngest granddaughter's birthday and my husband and I went to a large toy store to look at tricycles for her. We parked in the store's lot and I got out of the car and started walking towards the store.

My husband was walking a few feet ahead of me so he didn't see me step on a small rock on the pavement and begin to lose my balance. I staggered to the side and then felt myself falling. I probably would have cried out, but instead of being a hard swift fall onto the hot cement, it was as if strong hands were holding me and lowering me slowly to the ground.

My husband turned around and tried to catch me because he saw that I was falling towards the raised cement curbing surrounding a small tree. He was too far away to reach me. I saw the curb too and thought *if I hit that I'm a goner.* At the same time, I was still feeling those invisible hands, or maybe they were wings, that continued to support the weight of my body. When I did connect with the curbing something cushioned my head and shoulders and placed me down as gently as a mother placing a baby in a cradle.

Happiness Awaits You!

My husband's face was white with fear, but I sat up and told him I was all right. He helped me to my feet as other people came running over to see if we needed help. Although I have arthritis on my spine, I didn't feel any discomfort. I didn't even feel jolted from the fall. I told everyone that I was fine and insisted that we go into the store and look for my granddaughter's birthday gift.

Sometimes after a fall or other accident, the injuries are not immediately felt, but become more and more painful as time passes. I prepared myself for waking up the next morning with aches and bruises, but that didn't happen. I kept reliving the fall in my mind and kept feeling the strength of those invisible hands that kept me from harm.

A few months later, a friend who had been in a crash told me that he climbed from the wreckage and walked away because he knew that it was not his time to die. His words reminded me of my own experience and the angels that performed a minor miracle on a hot summer day in front of a toy store.

Carol Costa is a co-author of this book.

Ninja the Amazing Reading Therapy Dog
By Barry Reifman

I thought I would tell you about a success story. My wife, JoAnne, and I along with our German Shepherd Dog, Ninja vom Barendika C.D.G., TDIA, went to Lookout Mountain Elementary School in Phoenix, the school our children attended many years ago. We contacted the principal, who to our surprise was totally enthusiastic at the prospect of Children Reading with Dogs. We started the program the next week with Ninja visiting 2 classes, one was first grade children with reading problems, the second class was for children with emotional problems.

We were all very nervous the first day, including Ninja and the children. The children and I sat in a chair with Ninja between us. They read. We listened. They stumbled over words, some reading so quietly you could barely hear them. We helped when asked but mostly we listened.

Although we're not trained professionals, the improvement we noticed in the coming weeks was phenomenal. The kids practiced in our absence reading a book of their choice, and by the time we came on "our" Thursday, they were excited to read to Ninja. They were able to read out loud with confidence and very few errors, whatever book they chose. They took the time to sound out difficult words carefully. As the school year progressed I found the children picking books that were more and more challenging.

Ninja, who was unsure what to expect at first, now sits patiently or lies down with the children and lets them play with her feet and pet her gently. She'll lick their face if they stumble on a word, and kisses them gently on the arm or leg when they are finished. She doesn't mind if they kick their feet with nervous anticipation, or if they put their hand down her ear to exclaim, "Wow, I didn't know my hand could go down her ear that far!!" She accepts them with unconditional love and patience, a key, I am sure, to the success of this program.

The teachers are incredible, and have an amazing ability and attitude about incorporating the program into their curriculum. The kids now make up and write their own stories to read to Ninja, sometimes keep a diary about her visits, write letters and make drawings about her which they often generously give to us when we visit. They have even performed a play for the benefit of their friend, Ninja. Each class, as a whole, has written their own story about her.

It's been more than 5 years and we have gone faithfully every other week to both classes. In fact, we wouldn't miss a class unless an earth shattering event occurred. The program has been incredibly rewarding not only for the children who we help, but for us. When we leave our classes, we just feel plain good about ourselves for the rest of the day. It's the kind of feeling you should get from volunteering and helping people. It makes Joanne and I happy.

I suppose I could go on and on with the rewards of this program, but I'll leave you saying if anyone is thinking about trying Children Reading with Dogs, go ahead. You'll have a lifetime of good memories of helping children who, in turn, will hopefully have a lifetime of good memories of you and your special dog. Without a doubt, happiness can ome from our four-legged friends.

JoAnne and her husband, Barry Reifman have owned a full line pet shop and are now co-owners of No Stink, Inc, the "Home of OdorZout" all natural odor eliminating products. Please visit their website: www.88stink.com

Along with their pets, they both volunteer their time visiting hospice patients as well as participating in the Dogs Reading with Children program. See the YouTube video. Ninja the Dog Speed Drawing. JoAnne is also a jeweler featuring handmade silver jewelry that is "Everyday Wearable Art." Contact her via her website, www.Jewelrybyjo.com.

Moments: The Notes in Your Heart's Song
By Barry Goldstein

Like notes in a song, moments lead us into the chorus of our life…the chorus of a song is the part that we all sing along to, the part we all remember. Each moment is strung together to create a larger time period in our life and these larger time periods become our life… but the moments are the notes that create the song and the song is our life. It is the beautiful moments that create a beautiful life; a life so beautiful others sing along with it and are inspired to find the song of their heart!

The universal ripple affect has been one of the most profound truth's to affect my life.

It's simple to understand yet challenging to implement. Drop a stone in the water and the ripple moves outwardly from the center to create larger circles. Everything moves outwardly from our center as well, and our center is our heart.

It all begins with us, to create world peace we must create inner peace first, to find love in our lives' we must first love ourselves in our heart of hearts. And this love starts now, in this moment. There is no delaying, there are no criteria, there is no learning, and nothing you have to do. It is already here, a remembrance that can be re-ignited in this moment. And as you re-ignite it in your center it ripples outwardly and inspires others to do the same.

How do I re-ignite this remembrance that I am love? The answer is listen, listen to your heart. What makes your heart sing? Not, what am I here to do? Not, why am I not happy? What makes your heart sing? What brings you harmony? When do you feel like you have found your rhythm in the dance of your life? It could be a walk on the beach, listening to your favorite song, painting, writing or something you loved to do as a child. Close your eyes for a moment, put your hands on your heart, and just remember...

Make a commitment to nourish yourself everyday with something that makes your heart sing. In these moments of making your heart sing you begin to truly listen. These moments are the notes that begin to create your heart's song.

The moments link together to create the chorus of your life, the part that we all remember! The part that inspires others to inspire others to inspire others. Inspiration creates inspiration and it all starts in the moment!

Sometimes it is in the smallest steps that we find the largest movement. These small steps carry large messages that we send out. That we trust, that we know we will be supported, that we don't have to have all the answers. The space we leave for the answers to come in is where magic and miracles occur. May your life be filled with magical and miraculous moments and may many sing the chorus of your life!

Grammy Award-Winning Producer Barry Goldstein's musical experience spans many styles and genres from winning a Grammy with Les Paul for Best Rock Instrumental in 2005, to providing ambient music for Shirley Maclaine. Barry has composed for NBC, ABC, Fox and Lifetime Networks as well as being an award-winning composer for film. He has produced music for EMI, Polygram, Atlantic, BMG and many other major record labels and has worked with some of the hottest studio musicians in the industry! Please visit his website for more information: www.barrygoldsteinmusic.com.

A "Simple" Life of Happiness
By Susan Jeffers, Ph.D.

There was a time in my life I thought it was only "the grand splashes of brilliance" that would make me feel sublimely happy...graduation day, getting married, getting the great new job...and so on. In recent years, I have found something just as special as those grand splashes of brilliance...and I can have it every day of my life. I have found the beauty in the simple, ordinary everyday activities in my life...

a *simple* dinner with friends,

a *simple* walk in the neighborhood with my husband,

a *simple* evening watching television,

a *simple* day of creation at work.

a *simple* shower with the healing power of hot water...

and on and on and on...

The reason I derive so much pleasure from these simple everyday activities is that I have learned to be present in the moment...and *notice*. I have learned to notice the loved ones around me, and I feel blessed. I have learned to notice the food I have to eat, and I feel blessed. I have learned to notice the sunset, and I feel blessed. I have learned to notice all the gifts my husband brings into my life, and I feel blessed. Just noticing the gifts I am given every day brings joy to my heart.

I have also learned the art of *looking deeply*...of looking beneath the surface and seeing the miracle of it all. For example, at one point in my life I HATED going to the supermarket. It was something I rushed through so I could get to something more pleasurable. But then I learned to *look deeply* and all of a sudden shopping in the supermarket became a glorious experience. In **End the Struggle and Dance with Life**, I describe looking deeply in the supermarket as follows:

> As you walk through the door of the supermarket, just survey the rich array of products from which you can choose. Then, as you fill your basket with a dozen eggs, a loaf of bread, salad fixings, and a whole basketful

of other items, look more deeply and notice the huge variety you have to choose from--so many kinds of bread, so many kinds of greens, so many kinds of cereals, so many kinds of desserts. The richness of it all!

As you focus on the abundance in your basket, look a little more deeply and focus on the money you have to pay for your purchases. Even if you can't buy everything you want, you can still buy enough to sustain you. (Given the number of overweight people in our society, most of us buy more than enough to sustain us!)

Next, look even more deeply as you focus on the farmers who grew the greens that gave you your salad fixings and raised the chickens that gave you the eggs and grew the grains that gave you the bread and cereal. Focus on the bakers who baked the bread. Focus on the drivers of the trucks, captains of the ships, and pilots of the planes that transported all the riches to your doorstep.

Then look even more deeply as you focus on the staff that is there to serve you; some of them have been up since very early in the morning to set up the displays in a way to please you. Focus on the people who took a risk and invested their money to create a supermarket to provide you with such sumptuous fare. Focus on the people who built the building that houses the market.

Then look even more deeply and focus on those who created the roads that allowed you to drive your car to this place of wonder... and those who manufactured the car that gave you so much mobility.

Then look as deeply as you possibly can and focus on the ultimate Source of it all...God, the Force, the Universal Light...whatever it is for you, that created the air, the sun, the water, the earth, that makes all growth possible. One can't deny the miraculous rhythm and flow to it all.

Wow! Now you must admit that when you look at the supermarket in this way, it is a MONUMENTALLY LARGE GIFT that we have been given. And it becomes a joy to experience. A dear friend once gave me a poem by Emily Dickinson which included the following:

> As if I asked a common alms
> And in my wandering hand,
> A stranger pressed a Kingdom

Ah, yes! I went to the market for a tomato and, when I looked deeply, "a stranger pressed a Kingdom" in my hand.

You can see that by looking deeply in this fashion, it is possible to make the "must do's" in our lives a total joy to do...and you will smile with pleasure as happiness is placed in your hand over and over again. Yes, the "simple" events in our lives can be magnificent, indeed! And, they certainly make us feel happier in these difficult times.

Adapted from **End the Struggle and Dance with Life: How to Build Yourself Up When the World Gets You Down**

Susan Jeffers, Ph.D. is considered one of the top self-help authors in the world. The Times *(London) named Susan "the Queen of Self-Help." Her first book,* Feel the Fear and Do It Anyway®, *launched her career as a best-selling author. Seventeen more books and audio programs about fear, relationships and personal growth have followed, including* Embracing Uncertainty, Life is Huge! *and* The Feel the Fear Guide to Lasting Love. *Her books are available in over 100 countries and have been translated into 37 languages. Visit her website at www.susanjeffers.com.*

My Favorite Player
By Carol Costa

My love of baseball and my devotion to the Chicago White Sox began with my grandpa and play by play radio broadcasts. Although I was too young to understand the game, I would sit on the floor in front of the huge radio that provided most of the family's entertainment in those days and listen to the sounds of baseball. Bats cracking against balls, the roar of the crowd, and the voice of the announcer describing the action became an integral part of my childhood.

Sometime in 1947, my father brought home a miracle. It was called television. Now the sounds of baseball took a backseat to sights like the pitcher winding up for the throw, the base runner stealing third, and the ball sailing over the outfield fence for a home run.

As I grew into a teenager, I became more and more entranced with America's favorite past time. I knew every player on the White Sox team, the positions they played, and their battling averages. Long after my grandfather passed on, my sister and I remained avid fans.

Although the White Sox hadn't won a pennant since the infamous scandal of 1919, we knew that someday our faith in our team would be rewarded. It was the late fifties when hopes of bringing another league championship to White Sox Park were really soaring. It was a scrappy hit and run team with future Hall of Fame players like Nellie Fox and Luis Aparicio.

My sister and I went to as many home games as possible. Ladies Day at Comiskey Park meant ditching school or work to sit in the grandstands screaming for a hit or an out. When the game was over we hurried around to the player's parking lot to get autographs from our favorite players.

The player I wanted to meet the most was an outfielder named, Al Smith. The Sox had gotten Al from the Cleveland Indians and I thought it was the best trade the team had ever made. He was an excellent outfielder, often making unbelievable catches, and at the plate, his batting power drove in run after run for the team.

Our trips to the players' lot became a ritual. We got to talk to a lot of the team members. Our autograph books were filled with signatures, but the page I had reserved for Al Smith remained empty.

I would call out to the other players, "Tell Al Smith to come out here. Tell him his biggest fan wants to meet him." They all promised to give Al the message, but he never appeared.

In 1959, the White Sox finally did it. They won the American League Pennant. The city went crazy. Air raid sirens blared, fireworks filled Chicago skies, and victory parties broke out everywhere. We were so happy; we were literally dancing in the streets.

Everyone wanted an official team photograph, but they were hard to come by and my sister and I were not able to get one.

The Los Angeles Dodgers defeated the White Sox in the World Series and before the next season began, many of the Sox players were traded away. I felt like it was the end of an era.

I married and began to raise a family, so trips to the ball park became infrequent, but I still watched the games on television. Eventually, my husband and I moved our family to Tucson, Arizona. The Chicago White Sox were still my team, but I was no longer able to see them play and had to content myself with statistics in news broadcasts.

The years passed quickly, with four kids and a full time job, the only baseball I seemed to have time for anymore were my son's Little League games. In 1978, I got a real estate license and since my business background was in public accounting, I began working with real estate investors. A few months later, one of my accounting clients, a major real estate firm, asked me to become a part-time agent with their company. I went to their office to talk to the broker, who began telling me about some of the other agents who worked with him.

"Arthur Ashe's aunt works for us. And she's brought in another new agent, Millie Smith. Millie's husband used to play ball for the Chicago..."

Before he could finish the sentence, I jumped out of my chair. "Al Smith?" I screamed.

"Yes, I think so," he replied carefully.

I could see that he was rather startled by my reaction, but I was too excited to care.

"Where is she?" I demanded. "I have to meet her. Al Smith is my all time favorite player."

"Does that mean you're accepting the job?"

I nodded absently as I continued to babble. "Al Smith, how great. He was a fabulous outfielder and what a hitter, always came through in a clutch. I can't believe this." I had come a long way since my days at Comiskey Park, yet I was suddenly back to a time when a line drive over the center field fence brought me to my feet shouting for joy.

Millie Smith turned out to be a charming lady and we worked a few real estate deals together. Arthur Ashe's aunt taught me to doctor up bland restaurant offerings with the Tabasco sauce she always carried in her purse. But meeting Al Smith was the best, a dream come true.

My initial introduction to Al took place in the real estate office's parking lot. When Millie called him and said one of his biggest fans was in the office and wanted to meet him, he got in his car and drove right over. He was delighted to find someone in Tucson who remembered him and we became fast friends.

In the months that followed, I was able to spend time with Al, talking about baseball, the White Sox and his career. When I told him I always wanted his autograph, Al gave it to me on the official photo taken of the 1959 championship team. He even provided one for my sister.

Today the team photo with Al Smith's autograph is framed and hanging in a special place in my home. Al Smith has passed away now, but every time I look at the photo he gave me, it brings a smile to my face. It took me more than twenty years to meet my favorite player, but it was worth the wait. I'll never forget the thrill of meeting him and the minor miracle that caused our paths to cross.

Carol Costa is a co-author of this book.

The Spirit of Joy Resides in Cursive Writing
By Angeline Welk

Joy is that feeling that arises from your mysterious core when you are witnessing a colorful sunset, a bright rainbow, or a garden of flowers. In balanced handwriting, letters made with care are like flowers to admire. They represent a creation that comes from the warmth of the heart. In reality, the archetypal nature of each alphabet letter is colorful and has its own sound quality. They are unique flowers in their own geometric form.

The English letter Ss influences you to grace your life with joy. It reminds you that this quality boosts your immune system, cellular functions, and vitality. The letter Ss also assures you that peace, wholeness, and prosperity flourish when joy is your spirit.

This spirited letter prompts you to pursue work and activities that help you feel joyous. When you are deeply joyous, everyone benefits for your spirit is uplifting and nurturing. The letter Ss is a balancing letter. It reminds you to harmonize your triad nature expressed as empowered will, wisdom, and an active intelligence. These three aspects are the attributes of your core self.

The letter Ss encourages the spirit of joy to permeate family life, work environments, and healing centers. Its influence extends to all forms of education, reminding participants that learning, teaching, and sharing are rewarding when they come from a joyous nature.

Handwriting reminder: the design of the letter Ss appears as a printed Ss. The one difference in cursive is that you complete the fluid, balancing movement by ending to the right. Preferably, use the same style for both large and small letter Ss. The fluid, balanced, and graceful movement of this letter supports your inner and outer well-being. This potential is in your hand.

The Spirit of Joy Resides in Cursive Writing is part of a regular column on "Handwriting literacy" published by The Garden Island newspaper, Kauai, Hawaii

Angeline Welk is a trained writing therapist, author and educator who guides individuals to see their lives from a holistic perspective. She is a graduate of the International School of Graphoanalysis and has written a complete course on how to read handwriting. She can be reached via her website: www.ourlivingalphabet.com.

Dragonfly Transformation and Joy
By Danita Barton

Transformation, transition, shift in consciousness, it all means the same thing: change! We're all in the middle of a transition or transformation of some sort. Have you ever tried to remember when your transition began? That one defining moment that "kicked off" your whole transition process that changed your life, changed the way you look at things…that shift in consciousness. I believe I have pinpointed mine.

I went to Atlanta to visit my daughter for my birthday, it was a great trip. I turned 50! Well, I decided to embrace the day instead of grieving it; besides embracing it was decidedly more fun. At any rate, the point is that for months I had been having these moments of what I called psychic clarity, experiences in which I proved to myself that I have a gift.

I knew this gift, whatever it was, needed to be nurtured so I could grow properly, so to speak. What I'm trying to say is that I have had many wonderful experiences, but this was the first time I had a witness, my daughter. How awesome that I could share the day a dragonfly chose to speak to me.

My daughter, Desiree, and I were on our way to dinner. There was a dragonfly on her car antenna; he just parked himself there. Being a photographer at heart, I was excited and got the camera. I really could not see because of the glare of the sun so I decided to ask my daughter to take the picture for me; her eyes are much younger than mine. However, just as I had this thought, I was suddenly very focused and could see the dragonfly clearly. I took the shot. Amazing! To our surprise he stayed right there and let me take the picture. As I was taking the picture I noticed he was looking right at me. I started talking to him. I said hello and told him he was beautiful.

There was something about that moment, eye to eye with nature, which will stay with me forever. It felt as if he looked at me and understood. Talk about an "aha moment!" What happened next was quite astonishing. I tilted my head to the right; he tilted his head. I tilted my head in the opposite direction and he did as well. Of course I thought this was quite a coincidence, so I tried it again. I tilted my head to the right and he tilted his head. I tilted my head in the opposite direction and he did too. Each time he followed me.

I cannot fully express what that meant to me; it was a very moving moment. I got my daughter's attention, "Do you see? Do you see?" Of course she saw. She thought it was interesting, but it was her mom and did not surprise her. I was surprised at first, but it was I that felt the powerful connection! Incredible, the day I spoke to a dragonfly and he spoke back.

I have since learned the dragonfly symbolizes going past self-centered illusions that limit our growth and change. The dragonfly is a reminder that we are light and can reflect the light in powerful ways if we choose to. For me the dragonfly is a symbol of happiness, new beginnings and transformation, hope and unending possibilities.

I have never forgotten that experience. It stays with me each time I move forward on my spiritual path. Shortly after the experience, on a whim, I moved to Arizona. I was led to the Southwest Institute of Healing Arts where I enrolled as a full time student in their spiritual studies program. It has changed my life in more ways than I ever dreamed. The experience has taught me to assist others in discovering their journey, which continually assists me in my journey. I have discovered that as I help to heal others I also heal myself. My heart is open to give and receive love. As I go through my life now I have a sense of peace, happiness and joy.
I love dragonflies!

Danita Barton currently resides in Scottsdale, Arizona where she is in private practice as a spiritual healer with her close friend and partner, Lisa DeChiara. Danita & Lisa: Holding Sacred Space. Together they assist clients with Spiritual Coaching, Toe Reading, Angel Therapy, Traditional Reiki and Shaman's Touch healing, as well as, a wide range of other spiritual services that provide and guide their clients to a place of spiritual wellness.

Simple Pleasures
By Carol Costa

A friendly smile from a passerby
The sound of laughter, a lilting tune
A giant saguaro reaching toward the sky
The summer sun, the stars and moon

A child's hand clutched tightly in mine
The fragrance of flowers, the peace of night
A walk in the woods through crackling pine
Puffy white clouds, dawn's first light

The majesty of a mountain tall
A rippling brook, the ocean's roar
Turning leaves at the start of fall
The canyon where an eagle soars

A whispered prayer, a surge of hope
The miracle of a baby's birth
Simple pleasures that help me cope
Glimpses of heaven right here on earth

Carol Costa is a co-author of this book.

STEPPING STONES

Miracles are all around us.

Activity: What minor miracles have you witnessed or experienced?

_____

_____

_____

_____

Activity: Think of ways you can spread joy. What simple acts can become minor miracles to others?

_____

_____

_____

_____

Activity: Wherever you are, look around you. What do you see that makes you happy? Why?

_____

_____

_____

_____

Activity: Start a gratitude journal. Every day write down at least four things for which you are grateful.

_____

_____

_____

_____

CHAPTER 2

Feel the Love

The Power of Love, is there anything greater? Although the emotions of romantic swept-off-your feet love and lust can be nice too; there is a love that transcends most human emotions. This is that feeling that you get every once in a while that just comes flooding out of your heart so fast, so full, and so miraculously that you know without a shadow of a doubt that everything, absolutely everything, is right in the world. It not only feels right, it feels glorious, magnificent, blissful, and appreciative beyond words. This, some will say is God's Love, or Source energy, or Universal energy. Regardless of what you call it, it is something that can melt away a blizzard of ice around others. It is contagious, but only if.... and it's a big if, you allow it into your heart.

Do you feel that love? If so, how often? Do we close ourselves off to this deliberately at times? Is it something we do unconsciously? Do we even deserve to feel this good when there are, as we all know, malnourished children, war, disease, financial issues, traumas and dramas everywhere around us? Why should we feel this good when others are suffering? How dare we feel so glorious when the world is filled with problems? Are we meant to be miserable like those around us? Should we be feeling guilty because there is so much suffering in the world?

In the words of Marianne Williamson, spoken by Nelson Mandela in his inaugural address, "We were born to make manifest the glory of God that is within us. It is not just in some of us, it is in everyone."

The glory of God that is within all of us is his Love. Capital L. We have the power to let that light shine and brighten up the darkest of moments. But how?

As we fasten our seat belts on an airplane, a flight attendant stands in front and drones on about the safety features of the aircraft and what to do in an emergency. But in that little FAA mandated spiel, there is a wonderful analogy. When traveling with small children, remember to put on your oxygen mask first, and then assist others.

Put on your oxygen mask first? But what about the small, helpless child sitting next to you? Consider this: could you assist others if you are unconscious? Of course not. So it is with Love. It is important that we keep our hearts open to the Source of Love for ourselves first and foremost.

Take Care of Yourself
By Maggie TerryViale

I am a mother, and now a grandmother. There was a time I was so worn out, so frustrated with events around me, that I misguidedly took it out on my children by being short-tempered and yelling. I was out of balance. I was unconscious to Love. I was depleted. I had nothing left to give my children. I felt that I was following in the footsteps of my parents, and felt like a bad mother. I did not know then that I needed to take care of myself first, that I needed to put on my own oxygen mask.

I went away for awhile. Rested, relaxed, re-oxygenated myself by the sea of Love. I came back a stronger, more loving parent. Today my heart sings with love for my children and grandchildren, something I could not have done without nourishing my soul.

Maggie TerryViale is a co-author of this book.

Unexpected Friends
By Katherine Carol

The day started out like so many others over the last 18 years. It is a Sunday. I am deep in thought, planning my week, breaking down all the little jobs, clustering them and working them in between the gentle interruptions of my daughter. The knocking on our front door pulls my attention away from the confines of my thoughts. I open the door and am greeted with a jovial, "Hey, girl!"

It is Richard, my 70-year-old neighbor, a retired deputy regional FAA director, who happens to be gay. He comes in with all the confidence and swagger of a former pilot who is used to having his own way.

Yet, he is here checking in on us: a single mom and a young teenager who just happens to have charisma that pulls good people to her like a magnet. Richard is headed to the grocery store and asks if we need anything. Even if I say "No," he will bring something back for Mikelle. That is just the way he is. When he makes dinner, he will bring "extra" over; when he sees me looking a little haggard, he will say, "I am putting the coffee on—we need to talk!"

On those days, I fall into his big leather chair and hear his words of wisdom charge across the room with lightning-bolt accuracy. His piercing questions do not let me off the hook as he probes to take a deeper look at my circumstances. He is, with my permission, insisting I see the reality of the moment. His truth is often strong but loving. He counsels me to care for myself, redirect my energies and shuffle my priorities.

Gratefully, I have learned not to resist his directness as it results in more growth and perspective for all of us. I often lack the perspective necessary to see the forest for the trees. Mikelle uses a wheelchair as a result of significant cerebral palsy and I am her caregiver. I am at a point in life where I play superwoman, challenging systems to keep their promises to Mikelle and me, while also balancing a business and single motherhood. Richard is at a point in life where he has the time to listen, to share his wisdom and appreciate that he is appreciated.

It all began a few months after Richard moved to the second floor of our condo, just down the hall from us. Like many of our neighbors, he kept to himself—he actually was a bit of a grump. Mikelle and I decided to bake our fabulous butter crème-frosted sugar cookies for Valentine's Day. We filled little cellophane bags that were splattered with tiny red and pink hearts and we hung a bag on the door knobs of all the neighbors on our floor. Then we just forgot about it.

A few weeks later, Mikelle and I were backing her wheelchair into the waiting elevator and from around the corner came a booming voice, "Now, wait just a minute!" Turning around with surprise, we are face to face with this older, rather handsome man. He barks a question, "Did you leave those cookies on my door?" His suspicious manner was as palatable as an old, prickly cactus. I assessed the situation and simply said, "Weren't they delicious?"

He carefully looked us over, taking inventory of our situation, curious enough to ask questions about Mikelle's wheelchair and how she so deftly maneuvered it. Satisfied we were innocent enough, and not just "nosy neighbors", Richard also asked about her speech communication device. Mikelle quickly responded to his interest and started to show her stuff, asking him questions back!

It was an incidental moment colliding with fate—you know what I mean—a moment that signifies that our lives will change forever, our worlds so completely different and yet the same. Our friendship grew and Richard's understanding of what it was like to live with a disability deepened. Faced with his own health issues, his interest in Mikelle was in how someone could be so happy and yet experience such an extreme level of disability. With no small amount of irony, Mikelle had become the teacher as her grace and humor intriguingly offered insights into a world he had never seen.

Richard picked up on the unique rhythm of our life. He often jumped in with the nicest gestures to make life a little easier and less lonely. We laughed together over coffee and he and Mikelle developed their own relationship. He would tease her until she squealed with laughter and she would tease him back, and their banter would delight us all. On days I was away, she would even call him on her cell phone to come over and pick up something she had dropped on the floor. It felt so good to have someone looking after us after years of going it alone. And, after a few health scares, he knew he could count on us to be there for him.

Then the day came when there were no more knocks at the door. Richard realized Denver could no longer sustain his quality of life. He needed to breathe easier, go to a place where the elevation was lower and the climate warmer. He put his condo on the market and announced his decision to move to Palm Springs.

On the evening of my fiftieth birthday, he and Mikelle shopped for and prepared our special dinner like two kids up to great mischief. As we sat down to this lovingly prepared meal, he got the call from his realtor. His unit had sold. In seconds, our joy turned upside down and our emotions were tossed around like the salad on the table. Good news—sad news—tears filled Richard's eyes and he looked at me and then Mikelle, the silence briefly buffering the moment only to be shattered by Mikelle's sad and painful wail.

I knew our connection was strong enough to stretch across the country. But sadly our daily exchanges had to end when the final box lifted into the moving van and our lives forever changed.

Katherine Carol is an expert in transformation. She is not your typical motivational speaker or management guru. Her unique experiences give her deep insights into how systems work, the essence of personal motivation and of resistance. Her keen insights into our dramatically changing world landscape make her a bit of alchemist. Her methods for organizational and personal transformation have touched thousands and truly changed lives for the better. Katherine's approach creates a powerful path paved with realistic optimism, practical magic and a bit of focused effort to change lives and communities. She shares her strategies for savoring life, embracing adversity as a power teacher and methods to bring out the best in people, business and community. Visit her website: www.tangoresults. com.

I Choose Love
By Shawn Gallaway

In 1986 I was presented with a choice, to love myself and heal, or continue living my life with fear, and suffer the escalating consequences of disease and dysfunction. In choosing love, I began my healing journey. I opened my heart to the many layers of wounding I'd been carrying that kept me from being my true and authentic Self. Through the years I rediscovered my gifts in the arts and was able to transform my wounds into the light of peace I now embody. I began to live my life in service, thriving as a healing voice for Love on the planet. It's been a wild ride, one I wouldn't trade for the world!

I wrote the song *I Choose Love* two days after The Towers fell on 9/11. To me this event signaled a wake up call for all of humanity to the awareness that we have a conscious choice to make. Choosing love we create peace, choosing fear we self-destruct. It's that simple! Since then the song has been a tremendous tool for many on the healing journey back home to love. It reminds us that we do indeed have choice in every moment, and that right now we can respond to life's challenges with love to empower ourselves with the peace and joy we wish to see in the world. Love or fear, what do you choose?

I Choose Love

I can see laughter, or I can see tears
I see a choice, love or fear
What do you choose?
I can see peace, or I can see war
I can see sunshine, or I can see a storm
What do you choose?

Now I choose to live with freedom flying
From my heart, where the light keeps shining
I choose to feel the whole world crying
For the strength that we can rise above
I choose Love
I choose Love
I can see sharing, or I can see greed
I can see caring, or poverty
What do you choose?
I can see gardens, or I can see bombs
I can see life, or death
Coming on strong
What do you choose?

Now I choose…

I see us healing, the darkness dying
I see us dawning, as one world united
So what do you choose?
Love or fear
Oh, we choose

Now I choose to live with freedom flying
From my heart, where the light keeps shining
I choose to feel the whole world crying
I choose to feel one voice rising
I choose to feel us all united
In the strength that we can rise above
I choose Love
I choose Love
Oh, I choose Love

Shawn Gallaway is an accomplished singer songwriter with three CD's and one DVD to his credit to date. He is also an author and a gifted visual artist whose work has been shown through out the United States and abroad. As a workshop facilitator and a ceremonial healer Shawn has assisted and blessed many over the years with his keen insight and his ability to bring a sense of humor to the healing process. His current passion is combining all his gifts into a multi media theater production and film called The Choice. The Choice *can best be described as a healing experience that can enlighten and inspire the masses into loving action in the world through the use of the arts.*

Shawn's I Choose Love *CD and Book follows the soul's healing journey through pain, confusion and struggle to emerge into the freedom of self-awareness, purpose, compassion, joy, and connection. It includes songs, stories, and a series of original paintings that chronicle Shawn's own journey back to peace.*

Joy, Choose Joy
By D. H. Palmer

I personally believe that the foundation of my being is based in the spiritual and that I have chosen to experience the joy of this creative existence in the body I am in. Getting to know how to make the body, mind and soul work in a way that brings joy is part of my wonderful journey. There are so many quotes in the Bible and other religious texts that assure all of us that we are meant to go forth and flourish and enjoy. I have to believe that we just need to know how to take advantage of the secrets.

Learning exactly how to accomplish all that we are meant to do, be, and have can be joyful and rewarding, and challenging. I like rewards and I like to be happy. I want the positive emotions in my life as much as is humanly possible – the smiles, laughter, and any other feeling that registers in my core as positive and life affirming.

You can visualize your positive and not so positive thoughts in any way that works for you. I like sheep and goats so I picture them as positive and negative thoughts. I envision the flocks of thoughts racing through my head to be sheep. I stay with and nurture my good thoughts - my 'sheep'. Each time a negative or 'goat' thought pops into consciousness, I choose to let them go. Tend the sheep. Butt out the goats.

It is your spiritual self that has the power, and following that spiritual wisdom is vital to success in your journey. Remember the word created in your mind is the foundation upon which you build. Start simple. Work on picturing yourself healthy and whole. Only do those things that keep the body temple in the perfect shape it is meant to be in.

You have the power to create in your mind the perfect relationships you want in your life, whether in business or a personal relationship. See yourself blessed and joyous in all your relationships. Decide to attract people who bring harmony into your life. Listen to your inner wisdom when interacting with others. Whenever possible, choose to be with those who help you feel good.

Understanding the concept of non-judgment can help you tap into your built in guidance system. By not judging others, you are freed of many negative thoughts and emotions. See everyone as doing what they must for their journey. Love and accept them as they are right now.

Am I saying that if your child is taking drugs you should do nothing? Of course not. I am saying that from a place of centered calm ask your God spark mind spirit to guide you in constructive ways to help your child.

Meditation can release you from the need to judge life as good or bad, black or white. Meditation can help get you back to creating what you want. It is how you perceive life and what you do daily that will affirm your success or failure. No matter what is happening around you, think positive.

Ella Wheeler Wilcox's poem reminds us of the law of attraction and our power to create either positive or negative:

Thoughts are things, and their airy wings
Are swifter than carrier doves.
They follow the law of the universe
And they speed o'er the track to bring you back
Whatever went out from your mind.

Get into the habit of taking every opportunity to attract the positive, productive, and meaningful blessings you want in your life. As Grenville Kleiser said, "There is not a moment in which your character is not being shaped in one direction or another. Your life is simply the product of repeated choices. Grandeur of character is the effect of many habits. Know precisely what you want, proceed diligently toward it, and the best results will reward your diligence."

D. H. Palmer is a writer based in Tucson, Arizona. Obtaining a degree in Theater Production, she has utilized this knowledge to help others learn to tap into their creative powers. She has studied with many influential teachers in the self-help and new age movement and offers practical tips on creating a better life through the power of positive thought. She had the distinct honor and privilege to not only be at an intimate press conference the Dalai Lama but also had the supreme blessing of holding hands with him for a number of minutes. Along with a fellow self-help teacher and soon to be Unity Minister named Angel, D. H. Palmer offers workshops on how to create the perfect life you want, entitled, Scripting the Perfect Life.

Flowers for Susan
By Carol Costa

Like her unplanned conception, the arrival of my daughter was totally unexpected. Her three older siblings were getting ready for their respective performances in their school's Christmas show when I went into labor.

Her delivery went smoothly enough. My obstetrician was called away from his bridge game to perform the Cesarean Section that had been scheduled for the following Monday. "I guess this young lady wanted to pick her own birthday," Dr. Parker said cheerfully as a nurse brought the baby in for my inspection.

My husband stood beside me as Maria Lynn was placed in my arms. One look at her sweet face and my eyes filled with tears. "You're the best surprise I've ever had," I whispered.

The nurse unwrapped her blankets to show us that she did indeed have the right number of fingers and toes and then whisked her back to the nursery.

"I called home," Frank said. "Grandma and the kids are all delighted to have a baby sister."

"We're all very happy," I murmured just before I drifted off to sleep.

When I awoke the next morning, I found myself in a semi-private room in the maternity ward. The bed across from me was occupied by a young woman who introduced herself as Marcy. Her baby had been born two days ago, and she was getting ready to leave the hospital. We chatted as she gathered her things.

"This is my second child," Marcy told me. "She has a big brother at home. How many kids do you have?"

"This baby makes four, and I don't mind telling you that when I found out I was pregnant again after eight years, I almost went into shock."

"How old are your other children?"

"Christopher is twelve. Lisa is ten, and Joe is eight. Lisa has been asking for a baby sister for years and she finally got one."

"Sounds like you're going to have plenty of help with this baby."

"They're already fighting over who is going to hold her first when I bring her home from the hospital. I'll have to make a schedule."

Soon Marcy was on her way and Maria Lynn was brought into me for feeding. As I finished, Frank and the kids arrived. There were a lot of oohs and aahs over the newest member of our family. Then, Frank went out into the hall and returned with a huge vase of yellow roses. A white card attached to the flowers said, "To Mother and Daughter With Love."

"The flowers are from all of us," Joe told me proudly.

We were having a grand time letting each member of the family hold the new baby when a stern-faced nurse came in and took our guest of honor back to the nursery. Frank and the kids decided to go out to lunch. It was just as well. I was feeling some discomfort and rang for the nurse to give me a shot for the pain. I dozed off and on for the next few hours.

More flowers and plants began to arrive from family and friends. I nodded sleepily at the white-clad figure who said something about moving the roses to the window sill across the room next to the bed Marcy had vacated earlier.

Sometime later, the noise of a hospital cart and strange voices woke me. They were bringing another patient into my room. A woman with a harsh voice was speaking.

"Well, it's finally over with. Now we can put this whole ordeal behind us."

"Please, Mom," a young tired voice pleaded. "Don't call my baby an ordeal. Don't you even care that you have a granddaughter?"

"No," came the curt reply. "And you had better get those thoughts of keeping her out of your mind. If you think I'm going to support both of you, you've got another thing coming."

"I know."

"Then why haven't you signed the adoption papers?"

"Because I'm not ready to give her away yet. I haven't even held her."

"And you're not going to either. It will just make it harder to do what you have to do. Really, Susan, we've been all through this. Getting pregnant by a boy who doesn't care two cents about you was bad enough, but to even think of raising a baby at your age is ridiculous. You haven't even finished high school. You won't be able to get any kind of a decent job."

Susan didn't answer and her silence seemed to make her mother even more angry.

"All right," she yelled. "You've never listened to me. If you had you wouldn't be in the fix you're in, but I'm warning you…"

The woman's tirade was interrupted by a nurse. "Excuse me. You'll have to leave now. Your daughter needs to get some rest."

"Thank goodness," I whispered to myself. I had been pretending to sleep, not wanting them to know I was listening. I opened my eyes and caught a glimpse of Susan's mother.

She was about my age, dressed in stiff, black attire that matched her attitude and manner. "I'll be back to talk some sense into you later," she said coldly as she left the room.

As soon as her mother was gone, Susan burst into tears. The nurse tried to comfort her. "Come on, honey. Don't let her upset you. You're in a delicate way right now, but you'll feel better after you get some sleep. I'll be right back with the sedative your doctor prescribed for you."

The shift had changed and this sweet-mannered nurse had replaced the one who shooed my family out earlier. I was glad because my young roommate needed someone with a gentle touch right now. Susan sat up and began dabbing at her eyes with a tissue. She appeared to be about sixteen. Her short blond hair was disheveled and her face was the saddest I had ever seen. She suddenly realized that I was watching her.

"I'm sorry," she mumbled. "I didn't mean to wake you."

"It's okay," I assured her.

Before I could say anything else, the nurse was back with Susan's medication. She drew the curtain around the bed to administer the shot. I heard Susan cry out as the needle pierced her and she began to sob again.

She'll fall asleep soon, I mused. When she wakes up, I'll talk to her. She really seems to need a friend. I turned over on my side and closed my eyes again. The nurse was still behind the curtain trying to settle Susan down.

"Please, dear, try to stop crying," she said in a soothing tone. "Look, I'll bet you didn't even notice the beautiful roses someone sent you."

Susan's sobs ceased and my eyes flew open as I realized that the nurse thought that my flowers belonged to Susan. I started to call out to them, but it was too late.

"To Mother and Daughter with Love." The nurse was reading the card attached to the roses. "Someone must be very fond of you to send you such a big bouquet."

"There's no signature?" Susan asked. Her voice was hoarse from crying, but now there was a hopeful note in it. "I don't understand. How could I have gotten flowers so soon?"

"You were down in delivery for over twenty hours," the nurse told her. "Surely, people knew you were here. Someone probably called and found out what room you were assigned."

"Yes," Susan replied. "Kenny knew. He wanted to be with me, but my mother wouldn't let him come to the hospital with us. We knew our baby was a girl. He must have sent the flowers. He really does care about us." Susan's voice was growing softer as the sedative began to take effect.

My desire to reclaim the roses melted as Susan continued to speak, convincing herself that the flowers were for her. Despite her drowsiness her voice sounded excited, almost happy. "The flowers prove that Kenny cares about us, don't they?"

"Yes, of course they do," the nurse replied. "You get some rest now."

The curtain opened and the nurse looked over at me. "She so young," I said simply.

"According to her chart, the poor kid had a really tough time. She had to have an emergency C-Section. I always feel so sorry for girls like her. Having a baby should be a beautiful experience, but to someone like her, all the joy of motherhood often gets lost in the uncertainty and confusion."

"Her mother isn't very supportive," I said.

"At least the flowers were here," the nurse said,

"Yes," I agreed quickly. "I'm glad they helped her."

The nurse smiled and left the room. I sank back into my pillows. A few minutes later, Maria Lynn was brought in for her afternoon feeding. The nurse settled her into my arms and left us alone.

My little one was sound asleep, but as I eased the nipple into her tiny mouth, she instinctively began to take the nourishment I offered. I held her close and studied her perfect features. My heart swelled with love as I kissed her forehead and had the first of many talks with my youngest daughter.

"I let Susan think that our flowers were for her," I told Maria softly. "She's having a bad time right now and the roses made her feel better. You have so many people who love you, there will always be flowers for you. Even when things go wrong in your life,

I promise, you'll always have flowers."

Carol Costa is a co-author of this book.

STEPPING STONES

Love is a powerful force, central to our happiness. The more we love and are loved, the happier we are.

Activity: Make a love inventory.
How does love make you feel? How does love affect you?

_____

_____

_____

_____

Who gives you love?

_____

_____

_____

_____

Whom do you love?

_____

_____

_____

_____

What have you learned though loving others?

_____

_____

_____

_____

How do you express your love?

_____

_____

_____

_____

Are you missing opportunities to express love to those you care about? What can you do to be more loving?

_____

_____

_____

_____

CHAPTER 3

Can Anyone Hear Me?

Millions of prayers are uttered every moment of every day. Do ours get lost in the crowd? Should we keep asking when we don't seem to get any answers? It has been said that all prayers are answered, but not always in the way we expect them to be answered. It is also said that everything happens for a reason. If that is true should we just forget about asking for help and guidance in our lives? To answer that question we must remember that praying is a form of communication and the first thing you need to determine for yourself is who is on the receiving end of your prayer.

There are of course people who don't believe in a Supreme Being and therefore never try to communicate with that Being. Most people believe that there is a God and direct their requests accordingly. Whether you believe in God, Buddha, Jesus, or your own higher power consider that when you pray, why you pray and how you pray may affect the way your prayers are heard and answered. A good example of the when, why, and how of a prayer can be found in a true story about a man named, Joe.

In 1937, Joe had become an embarrassment to his family. He refused to hold down a job and spent all of his time drinking and gambling. One night in a strange city he was beaten severely by men who caught Joe cheating at the card game they were playing. Joe was thrown out into the alley. Unable to walk or see clearly, Joe crawled to a nearby transient hotel and passed out on a shabby mattress in a room filled with other men much like him. When Joe awoke the next day, he found that the room was pitch black even though the manager who wanted him out of the place claimed it was afternoon. Joe was blind, his vision taken away by the beating he had endured the night before.

For the first time in many years, Joe began to pray. He spent the rest of the day and the following night asking for help. "Please,

God," Joe whispered. "I'm young and strong and if you give me back my sight, I will work for you. I don't know exactly what that work will be; I'll leave that up to you. Oh, I know you've probably heard promises from guys like me many times before. And you're probably thinking that if you give me back my sight, I won't hold up my end of the bargain and go right back to drinking and gambling. But I won't do that, Lord. Give me back my sight and I'll spend the rest of my life doing your work."

Joe's story offers a prime example of when people pray. They turn to God as a last resort in a time of crisis. Joe's family had disowned him. He was in a strange city about to be thrown out into the street. He had no friends, no money, and no one who cared whether he lived or died. Why Joe prayed is obvious but perhaps the most important thing is how he prayed. Joe didn't just beg for mercy, he promised to change the way he lived and do God's work.

Perhaps his blindness was the catalyst that put Joe on the path he was meant to follow because Joe's prayer was answered and he regained his sight. As Joe had said in his prayer, some people would have gone right back to the things that got them in trouble, but Joe didn't do that. He kept the promise he had made. In Fairmont, West Virginia, the Union Rescue Mission started by Joe is still operating today. Joe spent the rest of his life helping people, like himself, rebuild their lives.

Prayer is a powerful tool, even if it is just used to reach the core of your own spirit and intellect. Whether you pray in a group, with a child, or alone in the darkness like Joe, prayer opens the lines of communication between you and the universe. Even if your prayers seem to go unanswered, they have served a purpose in your life, which may simply be acceptance and understanding.

God Doesn't Need Me
By Carol Costa

I had heard stories about people who claimed that their spirits could leave their bodies while they slept or meditated. Although I believed that it was possible, it had never happened to me until late one winter night as I was just drifting off to sleep. I don't know how others feel about leaving their bodies, but for me it was a frightening sensation. I thought my soul was on its way to eternity, but instead of heading towards the eternal light I remained there in my bedroom and received the following message: "God doesn't need me. I exist only through His love. His love for me spills over into my children and so it goes on and on. And when my earthly shell has turned to dust, I will still exist for all eternity, for I am God's love."

With the message firmly etched into my mind, I returned to my body with a lovely sense of peace and security and slept soundly through the rest of the night. I suppose I should have questioned why and how I received this message, but I didn't do that. I simply accepted the fact that it had been given to me for a reason. Did this message change my life or my beliefs? No, but it did change the way I prayed.

I usually prayed during my drive to work in the mornings. Maybe that's why I avoided accidents as I sped across town, trying to get to my office on time. After my usual prayer of thanksgiving for the blessings I have in this lifetime, I asked that those blessings continue and then presented my list of wants and needs to God. Now I realized that most of the requests I made had one common denominator and that was money. In one-way or another, directly or indirectly, I had been praying for money my entire life.

Now I reviewed what I already had and realized that more money probably wouldn't make me any happier than I was right now. Yes, it might alleviate some of the worry I had about meeting the needs of my children and paying our mortgage and other bills, but I had been thanking God all along for the blessings I had.

My husband, my children, my mom, sisters, and friends were not material or financial things, but living, breathing people who brought love, joy, comfort, counsel, and laughter into my life.

Changing the way I prayed did not keep illness and sorrow from my door or keep those unexpected bills from popping up, but it did help me cope, survive the bad times, and appreciate the good things in my life. My new prayer, one I use to this day, is: *Heavenly Father, I thank you for all my blessings. I place all my worries and concerns into your hands and trust in your love and mercy to see me through.*

Like everyone else in this country, I was terribly upset by 9/11. Our peace and security had been violated and our lives in the United States would never be the same again. A few days after the attack, my husband and I drove from Arizona to California and stood on a beach in San Diego.

As I gazed out at the vastness of the ocean, the message I had received so many years earlier came into my mind. I understood that my presence on this earth was no bigger than one of the billions of drops that make up the Pacific Ocean, but each drop and each person was part of a universe that could not be destroyed by acts of terror. Each of us is here because we are a manifestation of God's love, and love never dies, but lives forever.

Carol Costa is a co-author of this book.

All You Have To Do Is Ask
By Dee Wallace

It began as a simple adventure to our mountain cabin. My seven-year-old daughter, Gaby, and her friend were going to go on a girls weekend with me, trying to move on with some continuity after the death of my husband, Gaby's father. It would be the first time I would drive it on my own. It would be the first time walking in without Chris.

"I can do this," I told myself, "I can do this for her." On top of the anxiety I was already experiencing, a snowstorm was expected to hit en route. I had had the tires checked, chains checked, car fueled up. I was prepared. As we drove up the mountain to Lake Arrowhead, the snow began falling and the wind picked up. Driving became hazardous within minutes, it seemed.

"Please God, help me keep these little girls safe. I'm not used to doing this alone."

As we approached the final hill to our cabin, the car simply wouldn't make it. We'd get half way up, spin, and slide back down. I thought of leaving the car but all our provisions were in it. "Mom", Gaby yelled, "We can climb up the hill. We've done it a million times!"

All the options flashed before me. I suddenly recalled a back way Chris had taken before. "Could I remember it?" The snow was now coming down in blizzard strength. I decided to send the girls up the hill on foot with the cabin keys, and told them to wave off the balcony high above when they were inside. After what seemed to be forever, two smiling faces were waving back at me. "At least they're safe in the house; for now." I comforted myself.

I began the adventure of finding the back way. Everything looked so different in the snow and wind, but little by little I could recognize a house, a familiar sign, a storefront that looked familiar.

I eventually made it to a back street I recognized. I knew I was close but didn't know where I was. "I wish I could call them," I thought. But there was a lock on the phone for rentals. They couldn't get to me, and I couldn't reach them.

The car stalled. It wouldn't go forward and it wouldn't go back. The snow was falling harder and piling deeper. I got out to see if I could dig out. Not a chance. It was almost an hour and 30 minutes since I let the girls out. "They're only seven," I thought. "Please don't leave the house. Please don't turn on the stove, girls." I remembered how Gaby always wanted a cup of hot cocoa when we would arrive. How often I had let her "help" me make it on the stove. "Please, Gab, wait for Mommy." I could feel the panic slowly starting to rise up. I went to five or six doors. No answer. Gone or not rented this weekend. I looked around. I was lost. I was cold. I was alone. The street names seemed familiar but I had lost their context to our cabin.

By now my panic was full blown. "I have to get to those kids," I thought. I dropped to my knees in exhaustion and screamed out loud, "God! Send somebody to help me now!"

"Are you alright, ma'am?" As I turned to the voice, at first I was frightened. I had literally just combed the entire hillside. Not even a bird had been in sight.

"Please," I cried, "I'm lost. And my little girl is home alone. I can't find my way back. He asked me the address. I told him. A huge smile broke out on his face. "Why ma'am, it's right up there." As my eyes looked up, I saw the familiar corner and the bear flag that flew on the neighbor's porch. I had almost given up and I was only feet from being "home."

As my tears of relief fell, I turned to thank the stranger who had appeared from the empty forest, but there was no one there. And yet there was. "I just had to ask," I thought. "I just had to ask."

Dee Wallace has worked as an actress in film, television and on stage for over 30 years.   She's worked with Steven Spielberg, Peter Jackson, Wes Craven, Joe Dante, Stephen King and Blake Edwards on classics such as The Hills Have Eyes, The Howling, Cujo, The Frighteners, 10, Rob Zombie's Halloween, *and most notably,* E.T. The Extra-Terrestrial. *Dee has written three books devoted to the art of self-healing,* Conscious Creation, The Big E *and* The Spiritual Lessons of An Actor's Journey. *She conducts workshops to introduce people to healing techniques and facilitates private healing sessions. As a sought-after public speaker, Dee has spoken at numerous national and international venues. Her call-in radio shows airs worldwide (www. loaradionetwork.com/dee-wallace.html) Visit her website: www. officialdeewallace.com*

The Power of Prayer
By Denise K. Davis

I had this huge revelation about prayer about five years ago. I don't remember anymore what prompted it. I read lots of spiritual literature. I talk about spirituality with friends. I pray. Regardless, I remember my revelation was about how prayer works. Prayer is not about pleading or begging God to do something. In fact, those emotions of pleading or begging come from fear – and God does not know fear. God only knows love. Instead, prayer simply directs the energy of God to a particular situation. Imagine this: God has an infinite supply of healing energy available to all of us, all the time, for any situation. God does not interfere with our lives, so God will not do anything unless asked. Prayer, then, gives God's healing energy direction. That's it. And it goes there – to address whatever you wish. Prayer is the loving act of giving God's healing energy direction.

So many people believe prayers are not answered. They are stuck in their own ignorance of how wonderful God is and of how prayer works. They think if God doesn't grant a particular wish, their prayers have not been answered. Because we cannot see the Divine whole picture of our lives or of other's lives, we can misinterpret Divine doings. God is not interested in your interpretations of what is perfect for you. God is only interested in what is truly perfect for you. So, when you pray, don't ask for a particular person to love you – ask for the perfect person to love you.

When you pray for a job, don't ask for a particular job, ask for the perfect job. Don't pray to lose weight or to heal an illness, pray for God's perfection to shine through your body. And instead of praying to win the lottery, pray for God to bring you infinite abundance, in whatever forms that may take.

We can ask for guidance in any situation; we can ask for help with forgiving someone; we can ask for our hearts to be healed; we can ask God to expand our consciousness to help us know, more deeply, our divine connection. Be open and have faith.

Prayer works because God is Love and Love heals everything. Don't limit your definition of "healing" and don't limit God's magnificence. Stop trying to manipulate the physical world. Let God do that. Simply know that God is the source of all good in your life. Look to God, pray, and trust.

As much as we might want a loved one to heal from cancer or to walk again or to lose 100 pounds, our prayers must be for the healing of their hearts and souls, as well as their bodies – and for whatever is best for them. We do not know what their own path involves and if we direct God's energy to specific, physical outcomes we must do so with the proviso that we want what's truly best for that person in that situation. Sometimes what is best involves healing the soul but not the body.

That said, I do believe we can direct God's healing energy into the physical body to renew every cell, to heal every gland and organ and tissue – for their own good – whatever that means for that person. We direct God's energy and then we let go. We cannot be attached to the results. We have to respect that the results are truly best for the individual, regardless of what those results are and regardless of our own understanding.

The same holds true if we are praying for another to find love or to solve a financial crisis or just be happy. We can direct God's energy to that person, blessing them with love, and asking God to help them in these areas – according to their highest good.

Every time someone prays, God's energy is directed. The more frequently one prays, or the more people who pray, the more frequently that energy is sent. I like to picture beams of light coming from God to the person, animal, or situation being prayed for – flooding them with Love and healing everything and everyone involved. Just imagine - the unlimited power of Love – ready for each of us to use – waiting for each of us to change the world.

Happiness Awaits You!

Denise K. Davis received her doctorate in education from Teachers College, Columbia University and has spent her professional career in higher education, working with teacher training. She began pursuing complementary medicine and the body-mind-spirit connections to healing to resolve her own physical issues. This interest has turned into a second career and led to the writing of her book, Heal Yourself Thin, *and to her certification in energy work. She currently works as a consultant to help others achieve wellness.*
Visit her website: www.healyourselfthin.com

Wild Hope
By Ashleen O.Gaea

The coven was pretty typical: its members included a legal assistant, a salesman, a homemaker, a store clerk, a mechanic, and a nurse, among others. And the magic they worked on the full Moons was pretty typical too.

"The way it works," the priestess taught them, "is that we do everything we can to achieve our goals by ordinary means, and then we focus the energy of the universe on our need – knowing we don't have to deprive anyone else to satisfy ourselves."

She said, every time they met, "In ritual, we symbolize on the metaphysical plane what we want to manifest in our ordinary lives. We can call that activating the attention and power of our subconscious mind. We can call it asking the Goddess for help. And we can call it magic. It may not work the way we expect it to; She may not give us the answer we hoped for but She will always answer."

One month their magic was for the clerk's boyfriend to get a better job. They borrowed his pen and took turns circling likely prospects in the want ads, while they chanted "New job, better job, benefits; security!" By the next full Moon he was sitting behind a new desk, working for a company he liked, earning a higher salary and signed up for excellent health care coverage.

Another month it was to find a new airport for the salesman, after the one where he'd been landing his ultra-light closed. He stretched his arms out and pretended to be the displaced airplane taking off from the closed landing field. He ran around the ritual space, making "vroom vroom" noises and pretending to fly until he found a new airstrip, and then he landed again. The rest of the coven acted the parts of the new flight crew welcoming him to the new hangar. Within the month his little plane was parked at a field closer to his apartment.

This month, their magic was even more important. This month, their magic was to tip the scales from death to life.

The case had been in all the papers. A teen volunteer at a local charity's summer camp, in a meadow on a nearby mountain, had been terribly mauled by a bear. Part of her body had been devoured. The question of whether she'd ever walk again couldn't even be asked in the face of everyone's fear that she might not pull through.

The coven's nurse worked in the ICU at the hospital where the girl was being treated. That full Moon, she came to her priestess with a request. "Liz's parents have asked for everyone's prayers," she said. "I've got a lock of her hair here. Can we do some healing for her tonight?"

"You know we don't do magic for anyone, not even healing, without their permission," the priestess said. "But since her parents have asked and since they let you take a lock of her hair to strengthen our connection to her, yes, of course we can."

"We've camped in that meadow ourselves," the priestess added. "That will help bond our energy to hers. I'm glad we have this chance to do more than hope she makes it." Everyone was in agreement, and so they began.

A newspaper clipping from that day's paper, detailing the girl's dire condition, lay on the altar. On top of it was the blond, curly lock of Liz's hair. To one side was a bowl of water and a chalice; to the other, a bowl of salt and an incense burner. Toward the back, two candles burned, one for the Goddess who is the Mother of All, and one for the God, who leads us through each life.

When the Circle of worship had been cast, when Earth, Air, Fire, and Water had been summoned, and when the Goddess and God had been invoked, the nurse spoke. "Liz is near death," she said. "Her injuries are severe. She lost a lot of blood, a lot of flesh, and she's still in shock. Her parents have been advised to say their good-byes. She may not live through the night."

Wiccans don't usually wear time-pieces in their Circles, for their meetings with the Gods take place outside of ordinary time and space. But the nurse had come directly from her shift at the hospital, and still wore her watch. Its wide, luminous dial showed the time clearly: 8:37 p.m. Dutifully, everyone tried to ignore it, but their concern that Liz might die at any moment drew their attention to it anyway.

Without instruction from the priestess, each of the coveners took a strand or two from the lock of Liz's hair on the altar. The priestess started the chant, using the tune they all knew, but changing the words to fit Liz's need. "Live until the morning, live to be old and grey; greet thirty thousand mornings; greet your parents come the light of day."

Swaying slightly, they chanted until they lost count of the repetitions. Eyes closed. There were harmonies. Someone began to clap softly; someone else added another rhythm. They sang louder; they sang softer. Sometimes most of them hummed while one or two of them sang the words. Sometimes they held the strands of Liz's hair tightly; sometimes they stroked the strands with their fingers; sometimes they waved the tresses over their head like victory banners.

Finally, the chant began to fade, and they opened their eyes. Their priestess held up one finger; this was the cue. They were silent for the space of one heartbeat, and then raised the chant once more, strongly, commandingly, willing the girl to recover at that moment.

And when the nurse reached to put her strands of Liz's hair back on the altar, no one could help noticing the soft glow of her watch dial again. It was 9:22 p.m. After a few deep, grounding breaths, they concluded their service in their usual way, and left for home about an hour later, feeling productively exhausted and renewed at the same time.

The next morning, the nurse called her priestess. "I saw Liz's chart today," the nurse said. "Her blood pressure bottomed out at 8:40 last night, and they thought they'd lost her. But before they could do anything, it started coming back up, and by 9:20 it was normal again." She lowered her voice; she was calling from work. "That's right when we were doing our healing chant for her."

Yes, the coven and their magic was pretty typical; and yes, She will always answer.

Epilogue to this story: Liz made a full recovery, graduated from college, and now works at a veterinarian clinic.

Ashleen O.Gaea is a Tucson author and Wiccan Priestess who has published several books about Wicca, including, Family Wicca, Raising Witches, *and two volumes of* Celebrating the Seasons of Life. *She is breaking into fiction in 2010 with a trio of books:* The Green Boy, The Flower Bride, *and* Maiden, Vampire, Crone. *Visit her website: www.AshleenOGaea.com*

The Cabbage Patch Doll
By Carol Costa

My daughter, Maria, was five years old, a bright bouncy little girl with solemn brown eyes, and a smile that could melt a glacier. Maria was often referred to as my "surprise child" since there was an eight year gap between her and her closest sibling. This time span also accounted for the fact that Maria usually managed to get whatever she asked for, if not from her father or me, from her big sister, one of her older brothers, or her Aunt Marilyn. Luckily, Maria was a sweet-natured child who remained unspoiled despite her privileged position in the family.

On this particular day my nephew, Donnie, was visiting from Chicago and the Arizona sunshine had suddenly dissolved into torrential rains. I was looking for an indoor activity for that evening. A man I worked with came to the rescue with four tickets to a benefit being held at a local dinner theater. It sounded like fun, and since my husband was working that evening, Aunt Marilyn and I took Donnie and Maria to the benefit.

While dinner was being served, a few people moved from table to table selling raffle tickets for a drawing that was to be held during the theater intermission. Set up on a table across the room were a number of prizes donated by local businesses for the raffle. It didn't take Maria long to fix her eyes on a Cabbage Patch Doll, which at that time were hard to come by, and very much in demand.

"I want that doll," she announced. "Please can I have it?" she implored, looking from me to her Aunt.

"We can't buy you the doll," I explained to Maria. "We have to win it, and with all these other people buying tickets we don't have a very good chance of getting the doll."

Marilyn waved at one of the raffle ticket sellers and purchased five tickets. "When you win the doll, can I have it?" Maria asked her aunt.

"Yes, but your mother's right. There's not much chance of us winning, so don't get your hopes up."

Maria quickly lowered her curly head, and looked down at her plate. She ate her dinner in silence, and I assumed it was her way of showing her disappointment. After dinner we went into the theater to see the show. Our table was right down front, directly in front of the stage. The show was a rollicking farce with lots of laughs, but it was a little too adult for Maria. I thought she might get bored and fidgety, but she sat quietly while the rest of us enjoyed the show.

At intermission, the lights went on in the theater and the drum containing all the raffle tickets was wheeled on stage. There were at least two hundred people in the theater and the drum was crammed with tickets.

"I want that Cabbage Patch Doll," Maria told us again.

"I know you do, honey," I replied. "But you're probably not going to get it."

"Yes, I am," Maria declared. "Ever since I saw it, I've been asking Jesus to let me win it."

Now I understood why my little bundle of energy had been so quiet all during dinner and the show. Marilyn and I exchanged a look, and shook our heads at each other. Donnie just shrugged. He was the closest one to the stage, so Marilyn handed him the raffle tickets to monitor.

The drawing began and one by one the minor prizes were distributed. Donnie still held our five tickets, which so far had gotten us nothing. The final two prizes were a clock radio, and the Cabbage Patch Doll. The winning number for the radio was read, and Donnie let out a cry of surprise. One of our tickets had won.

There was a brief smattering of applause as Donnie claimed the prize. Marilyn and I exchanged looks once again. Drawing one of our tickets out of the hundreds in that barrel had been a real stroke of luck. However, the chances of another of our tickets winning the most coveted prize, the Cabbage Patch Doll, were next to impossible.

"And now for the final prize," the announcer said. He held up the doll and I dared to look over at Maria. She was sitting with her eyes tightly closed and her tiny hands clasped in prayer. Once again, I gazed around at the theater filled with people, feeling helpless. It didn't even occur to me to utter a prayer of my own. I was too busy trying to think of words that would soothe Maria's devastation when someone else walked off the stage with that doll.

Donnie was so startled to hear another one of our numbers that he jumped, causing his chair to topple over backwards. Marilyn and I were too stunned to move. Maria opened her eyes and stared at her cousin who was regaining his balance. "Who won?" she asked innocently.

"You did!" Marilyn and I shouted in unison.

Donnie handed Maria the winning ticket and lifted her onto the stage to collect her prize. She hugged the doll and twirled around in delight, while the audience gave her a thunderous ovation.

"Oh ye of little faith," I whispered to Marilyn.

Today, Maria is in graduate school studying law. The Cabbage Patch Doll is faded and worn, packed away with other childhood treasures, but in my mind that doll is as bright and clean as my memory of a delighted child claiming a wonderful prize. That image will always fill me with hope and remind me that when the odds seem hopelessly stacked against us, a little faith and a simple prayer can make us winners.

Carol Costa is a co-author of this book.

STEPPING STONES

Think of prayer as a conversation with God. Realize as you pray that God's love is infinite and unconditional.

Know that every prayer is truly answered and be open to whatever answer appears. To remind you of this, write down times when you have received an answer to your prayers that was not what you thought you wanted, but turned out to be the right things for you.

_____

_____

_____

_____

Pray with love (not out of fear) to direct God's healing. Take the time before you pray to count the blessings you have in this lifetime.

_____

_____

_____

_____

Know that love never does harm but sometimes teaches us the lessons we must learn to attain peace and happiness. What are some lessons you know you must learn?

_____

_____

_____

_____

Accept the answers that result from your prayers.

CHAPTER 4

Joy in the Workplace

What a delight it is to find someone who is truly happy in their work -- someone who clearly feels competent, who relishes the opportunity to use their talents and who feels fulfilled in what they do. Even better if they are valued for their contributions and compensated accordingly.

It's uplifting to meet people who identified their passions and pursued them, professionally. Whether it's a skillful dentist or a talented plumber or an inspiring teacher, they are constantly creating situations that bring themselves, their colleagues and their clients happiness.

Sometimes, there's a fairly direct route to a joyful career. More often, however, the path is more circuitous. Budding artists, for example, are often nudged in the direction of more lucrative professions when they are young and susceptible to the preferences of their parents or society. But true passions refuse to lie dormant forever and when they surface, they often point to alternative work outlets –- ones that are more closely aligned with a person's true nature.

Sometimes, career changes are mandated by external forces. It's not pleasant getting fired or laid off but one benefit of economic downturns is that it gives people the opportunity to completely change their career trajectory to something they really love to do.

Whether it's a bank teller, a veterinarian or a shop clerk, you can sense when you're interacting with someone who truly enjoys their work. Their happiness is infectious.

For some people, however, this is not the case – the job isn't particularly satisfying, employees aren't treated well or relationships with colleagues are not ideal. They've made sacrifices for practical reasons and they are stuck with their lot in life.

Or are they? With a little creativity, even mundane jobs can be become a source of happiness. If you can't change the work, you can change your attitude about it – you can find elements of the situation about which you are grateful. If you can't change your co-workers – and alas, you can't – you can change your attitude towards them and about them.

Working in Fantasy Land
By Lisa Rothstein

In 2003, I was an advertising creative director with a wall full of awards, a fat paycheck, a wardrobe full of good meeting-appropriate attire, and, best of all, an assignment in Paris, where I had been living and working for almost ten years. Ever since college, where I'd been recruited as a copywriter by Young & Rubicam, I'd never had to worry when anyone asked what I did. But now, the constant pressure and lack of meaning in my job was wearing on me.

I was single, had many talents and was wondering what else there might be to life. And I had really lost interest in my work. This is fatal in a job where getting others excited enough about fabric softener, tampons and laundry detergent to open their wallets is supposed to be the main focus of one's talents and passions.

I found myself fantasizing about ways of dismembering the cutesy teddy bear, the fabric softener's mascot, in my latest ad campaign. I came in to the office later and later. Lunches got longer. In France, neither of these habits is unusual, but I knew that for me it meant impending burnout. So I was relieved when another agency merged with ours, and I was asked to take a pay cut or be downsized. Needless to say, I chose the latter

Now free to do as I liked, especially with the help of the French system's generous unemployment scheme. I was drawing more in benefits than most of my friends were being paid working full time. I set about charting my next move. The trouble was, I was lost in the fog of a full-blown identity crisis. I didn't want to be an advertising executive anymore, but without my business card to tell me who I was, I simply didn't know.

The creative projects I always promised myself I'd tackle "when I had the time" still weren't getting done. Absent the structure, pressure and deadlines of my job, things like laundry and opening my mail were taking the whole day. I was rudderless, brooding and depressed. If I'd taken up smoking, I could easily have passed for French.

The one bright spot in my life was Thursday nights and Sunday mornings, when I sang with the choir of the American Cathedral in Paris. I've always loved singing, and this group was the best and most challenging I had ever been in. We did everything from 8-part Renaissance motets to complicated atonal modern pieces. Many of the singers were paid professionals, and sometimes, when they needed an extra alto voice for a wedding or a funeral, they asked me.

One day after such a wedding, at a castle in the Loire Valley, one of the pros mentioned that he was singing at Disneyland Paris for the holiday season, November and December, and that his group could use an alto. Was I free? Having loved all things Disney since birth, I smiled. I was amused by the improbable idea of trading in my business suit for a Technicolor Charles Dickens-inspired bonnet and petticoat and fa-la-la-ing a couple of months away.

I hesitated for a moment, thinking of my professional reputation. What if one of my old colleagues should see me? What would I tell my parents, who were still mourning the loss of my former status and their accompanying bragging rights? Their daughter, the Ivy-League graduate who once had an office on Madison Avenue was going to be a Disney character? But I certainly had nothing better to do right now. So I agreed.

It wasn't until I arrived at Disney that I found out that the group I had been hired for was not the Charles Dickens carolers, but an acapella jazz sextet called the Swing Along Santas. My costume was not a ruffled petticoat, but something in bright red fleece resembling pajamas with feet, with hoops inside the tummy to give me a Weeble-like figure. It didn't stop there. The suit was studded with Christmas lights operated by a ten-pound battery pack sewn into the back activated by a switch in the pocket to be turned on during *Rudolph the Red-Nosed Reindeer* and topped with a red nose and a Santa hat. And I was supposed to sing and dance in this getup?

I got the surprise of my life. It was the best job I'd ever had. I found I loved not caring about looking silly. I loved getting a behind-the-scenes look at a Disney park, especially eating in the employee canteen, where I might be eating beside Goofy, his head on the chair beside him. I loved being in the next locker room down from the Edelweiss Oom-Pah Band, whose bright green lederhosen made them look almost as ridiculous as we did. I loved the close harmony, both musical and personal, that I had with my singing teammates. And most of all, I loved getting out in front of the park guests, especially the children, mugging and trying to get them to sing and dance along with us. I'd ride home on the train at the end of the day, cold, exhausted and happy, not believing I was getting paid for this.

I knew that this would all come to an end in January. I also knew that it would never be my career. Singing Christmas songs in a funny costume isn't really a transferable skill. But I did find some transferable joy on that job. I saw that there were aspects of it, the things that made me love it most, that I could bring to almost any activity, career or project, and that I hadn't been consciously applying in a long, long time.

Here are my "transferable joys" from being a Swing-Along Santa at Disneyland Paris:

I didn't take myself too seriously. Even if I'd tried, it was impossible in that dopey Santa suit. Ironically, this was the only paying job I've had where I was actually on stage, and yet it's also the only job where I didn't feel and act as if the whole world depended on or revolved around me. I had some funny business to do during the skits and even a few vocal solos, but I wasn't trying to be the star, and nobody expected me to be. What a relief! And yet, I found people noticed and liked me just as much; in fact, probably more.

I did my job every day to the best of my ability, gave it my all, and at the end of the day "left it at the office". If I missed a note or a step, I let it go. I didn't berate myself, or allow myself to think that a mistake meant that I'd spoiled everything or that I had no talent. Nothing seemed a big enough deal to be worth worrying about.

I did, however, find myself replaying the fun or comical moments of the day on the train ride home and getting an extra smile or chuckle out of them. This was a big switch from my previous habit of reviewing my failures, wince-inducing things I'd said and various petty grievances…while discounting anything positive.

I showed up on time. There was no question of letting my team down, and the trains ran on a set schedule, which helped. But sitting on that train, I knew the peace of knowing that I would arrive when I was supposed to, with no adrenaline, no drama, no having to think up lame excuses, no reproachful looks. And no more trying to fit in "just one more thing" before I left for work. I gave myself permission to do less. And I felt that I counted more.

I put my whole self into what I was doing. Instead of sitting immobile at a desk for hours as my mind darted and bloated with obsessive thoughts, I was totally consumed by singing, dancing, smiling, turning on the lights on my suit at the appropriate time…there was no room for any distractions.

I was always looking around for more ways to have fun and enjoy life on that job. Granted, it was Disneyland, and fun was kind of the point of the whole place, but the main reason I was happy was my attitude. I was grateful to be there. There were some others there who looked quite Grumpy after they had placed their Happy head next to them on the banquette. They didn't seem to know or care that they were in the happiest place on earth. They looked like they were working for the IRS.

I liked most of the people I worked with and went out of my way to help them and be friendly, whether they were in my department or not. And as for the ones I didn't like so much, I didn't dwell on it. I got on with them as best I could. I didn't talk about them (ok, not much) behind their backs.

I didn't look to the work itself to make me happy. God knows the 150th time you sing *Rudolph the Red Nosed Reindeer* you've exhausted any inherent musical interest. The work was, by definition, routine to the point of monotony. But it was new to every audience who saw us, and that's where my focus went. I got out of myself and thought about others and making their experience a happy one. This made my energy an ever-renewable resource, no matter how many verses of *Jingle Bells* we had to sing.

I was proud to work for Disney, my uniform notwithstanding. I think I bought every item of Disney gear available and for a while I didn't own a pair of socks or underwear without a character on them. I now think if you work anywhere that you don't believe in what the company is doing, or in any profession that you have to make excuses for, you should get out immediately. I don't care how good you are at your job, or how much they are paying you. This is true even if –especially if --you have your own business. If you can't be proud of what you're doing, stop.

When I remember to apply these principles and practices to the work I do now, whether it's for a paying job, a volunteer post, or a personal project, I have a lot more joy in my life, and – not coincidentally – I find that the work goes better, too. After so many years as a successful executive, I'm so grateful that I got off my high horse, out of that corner office, and into that silly red costume. I found my true self again, and my sense of enthusiasm, doing the silliest, most unexpected job imaginable. Now I value having the right attitude as much or more as the right skill set.

And now, when I find the old dark clouds of stress and self-criticism beginning to gather, I hum a holiday tune, do a little dance, and everything lightens up. It does get me some odd looks in August, but I guess that's just an occupational hazard I'll have to live with.

Happiness Awaits You!

Lisa Rothstein has been a copywriter and creative director at Young & Rubicam, Ogilvy and Lowe where she created campaigns for IBM, Hanes, Johnson & Johnson and other Fortune 500 companies. An award-winning screenwriter, Lisa is represented by The Bohrman Agency in Beverly Hills. See http://www. YourWriterForHire.com. Lisa has also been a street performer in New York City, a standup comedian, a cartoonist and a voice-over artist. She still sings, now in much more tasteful attire, with the San Diego Master Chorale. Most recently, as a certified coach, Lisa has been helping other creative professionals reach their goals. Visit her website: http://www.TheDaVinciCoach. com

It's Better to Have Loved
By Liisa Kyle

Love is the secret ingredient in any good Guide Dog. You can't foster a Guide Dog puppy without getting pretty darned attached. It starts the moment the organization's official places an eight week old pup in your arms. Having been shipped across the state via Puppy Truck – a customized kennel on wheels – the dog is a bit dozy. His tiny lashes blink in the sudden sunlight. His petite, pink tongue licks your cheek, tentatively. As you stroke his silky Labrador fur, his little heart pitter-pats against your rib cage.

In short, it takes about three nanoseconds for the bonding to begin. Within ten minutes of meeting, you're so besotted with the dog that you don't mind the next month of potty-training and sleep deprivation. The subsequent year or so of training and nurturing your pup zips by faster than you can imagine.

Unlike raising a typical puppy, you are always aware that this beloved creature will be leaving you in the not-too-distant future. Even if you wanted to forget about the inevitable departure, you can't because every day at least three people will ask, upon meeting the dog, "How on earth can you give him up?"

When it's time to bid farewell to the pup you've fostered, it's not easy. It hurts. You grieve their departure. It doesn't matter if you have a month's notice (as we did with our first pup), a week's notice (as was the case with our third) or no notice whatsoever (our second pup was sent to the main campus for allergy testing and, to our shock, was placed with another raiser family in a different climate so we didn't even get to say 'goodbye').

Yes, the pup you've fostered is going on to bigger and better and more important things. The dog will be serving the greater good –- changing someone's life in profound ways. That doesn't change the fact that you are losing a family member with whom you are emotionally bonded. When the pup leaves, your heart breaks and your nest is changed forever.

And no, it's not akin to sending your kid off to college. Alas, dogs can't phone you or text you or post their status on Facebook. When you say goodbye to the pooch you've raised, all contact is severed for the duration of their training. Maybe forever.

Now it might be, as it was in the case of our first pup, that your dog graduates as a working Guide Dog. Through an extensive matching process, your dog is paired with a recipient with whom they undergo several more weeks of training as a team. That person then decides the level of contact you will have with the pup you fostered, if any. Most choose to take their new dog and take their leave.

My husband and I were fortunate that the first pup we raised, Cody, was paired with someone committed to keeping us updated on his life. Through regular, detailed emails, we still feel that Cody is in our lives, albeit a thousand miles away.

Our second pup, Elijah, didn't fare so well on campus -- making it through only eight of the ten final phases of training. (Of course they don't call it 'rejected' or 'failed', the preferred term is 'career changed'). In this situation, the pup's raisers get first dibs on the dog. When we received the call that Elijah would not be a Guide Dog, I interrupted the news to blurt out, "We'll take him! When can we pick him up?"

"Not so fast," said the Guide Dog official. At the time, my husband and I were training a very challenging pup named Pepper. "If you want Elijah, we'll need to place Pepper with another family. Pepper requires somcone's undivided attention. You can't have both dogs. Choose the one you want."

It was in this moment that we discovered that there is something much more difficult than sending the dog you've fostered away for his final training. Worse still than discovering that the dog you sent up to campus for a week of allergy testing was being transferred to a new family in an undisclosed location. We were now facing a Sophie's Choice decision that I wouldn't wish on anyone: we had to choose between two family members, Elijah and Pepper.

Truthfully, it shouldn't have been that difficult of a decision: Pepper was a pain. We called him El Diablo and no-one who met him wondered why. He was aggressive, naughty, stubborn and vocal. He hated the car and balked like hell whenever he was asked to get in (which is several times a day in the life of any Guide Dog pup). It's not cool to be seen in the supermarket parking lot, wrestling a Guide Dog vest-wearing puppy into your car. Every day, I feared that the Guide Dog organization would get anonymous tips from concerned passersby "Someone's trying to abduct one of your pups!"

Yet despite his challenging nature, we loved Pepper just as much as we had loved Cody or Elijah. We were just as deeply bonded. The decision shredded our hearts in different directions: what was best for Elijah? For Pepper? For us? It was an agonizing week. Sobbing, I consulted with more seasoned raisers about every conceivable option.

It came down to the fact that Elijah had been bred, raised and trained to be of service. We decided that if he could become a different kind of service dog, then that's what he should do. He was assessed by Hearing Dogs but found to be 'too much dog'. Dogs4Diabetics snapped him up, however, and this is where Elijah found his true calling. He would be paired with a diabetic person and go everywhere with them, much like a Guide Dog. He would learn to 'alert bark' when he detected aberrant levels of blood sugar in his person – even if the person was asleep (in which case it would be his job to wake his person and pester them until they took action). In the case of diabetic children, he'd be trained to go get a parent or teacher when needed.

As part of Elijah's training process, he was placed with a foster family that included a diabetic child. On one lakeside holiday, the kids were playing in the water. Elijah performed his 'alert barking' but failed to get the adults' attention. So he jumped in the lake, swam out to the diabetic girl, grabbed her by the life jacket and swam her into shore where he repeated his 'alert'. Her parents then determined that her blood sugar had dipped dangerously and Elijah cemented his life's purpose as a Dog4Diabetic service dog.

In the end, we seem to have made the right decision. Elijah was destined to perform life-saving heroics while we continued working with the terror known as Pepper.

We spent the next eight months working through Pepper's issues. We taught him to get into the car without a fight. He ceased yodeling. He was still pretty dominant and very stubborn but he became a loving, affectionate little boy who enjoyed snuggling more than any Lab we've ever encountered.

Yesterday, we got the call that it's time for Pepper to begin training in Oregon; this weekend! The time for separation grieving is nigh and condensed into a few scant days. Each time I look at his furry little face, tears well up. When I gaze into his distinctive almond eyes, something painful catches me right in the solar plexus. When he snuggles against me, I think my chest might burst.

This is what I've learned in the course of fostering three service dog pups: Love is inevitable. And love hurts. But I'd rather know love and the pang of its loss than never having felt those bonds at all.

Liisa Kyle is a co-author of this book.

When You Wish Upon a Star
By Katherine Metcalf

Remember that song? Jiminy Cricket would start off the Disney show with that song. I bet you can hear it in your head. Go ahead, take time right now and sing it or whistle it; I bet it makes you smile. It says that anything your heart desires will come to you. This song has been my mantra for many, many years.

As a child, I was a dreamer, an artist and a free spirit. At Halloween, my mother would take me to the five and dime and show me the pretty princess costumes sitting neatly in a box, yet my insides were screaming, "Please let me be a witch this year."

I was totally happy when I did get to wear the flowing black dress with the pointy hat and carry my magic broomstick. I would practice my cackle and twirl around, knowing that I had the power to illicit a lot of candy.

At 10 years old, I was the social coordinator of the neighborhood. I organized all the kick the can games and raised money for Jerry's kids. I also created a community newspaper. When I had alone time I would read books about incredible women like Amelia Earhart and Rosa Parks. I respected that they went against the rules of society and bravely lived their authentic life. I decided then that I would live life like that.

At the age of 13, I was fascinated with the stars, planets and Greek Mythology. All those books introduced me to the study of Astrology. I owned "the bible" of Astrology; Linda Goodman's *Love Signs* at the young age of 16. All of my girlfriends came to me for astro-love advice. I would spend hours reviewing their Sun, Moon, Venus and Mars to see if they had chosen the right boyfriends. I loved helping my friends and being the one with the answers.

At 17, I was starting to think about college, about what I wanted to be when I grew up I loved Astrology, but no one had a degree in that. So, I decided on the next best thing. I would be a psychologist.

At 18, my craving for something new took me from the rolling green fields of Iowa to the desert of Arizona. The sun and mountains called to me. (The cute tan guys in their puka shell necklaces didn't hurt either.) I started out studying Psychology then found out that the psych program at ASU was very clinical. I would have to work with rats-Yuk. There was no way I was going to work with rats. So I switched my degree program to Art and went back to Iowa.

I continued to study Astrology and do charts for friends. I also became fascinated with Reincarnation, Numerology and Tarot Cards. I could hear Jiminy Cricket singing in my ear again as the dreamy, artsy side of me emerged.

I graduated from Iowa State with a BA in Art. I was really proud of this accomplishment. I would finally fit into society. As I boldly entered the workforce

in my navy blue pumps with my resume in hand, I was shocked to learn that my BA would land me a minimum wage job. Oh my God.

Thus began my 20 year search for happiness in a career. The bad news, I went through 17 jobs in 3 different careers. The good news, I FOUND IT.

And you can find it too.

After several jobs where I quit or was fired, I realized that I really don't like being told what to do, how to do it or when to do it. I need to be the boss. I need to be the Queen Bee. But then the question arose, the boss of what? I needed to have my own business. But I also needed to pay the bills. So, I kept my job as a Food Broker-which was fun, kind of like show and tell with food. But I wasn't fulfilled, I kept having this nagging thought in my head: Why can't I do work that I love? Why can't I make a decent living without selling my soul?

I tried many multi-tiered marketing programs like Amway and Melaluca that promised riches; which I never acquired. Then I thought why not use my Art Degree. I created a whole line of designer marbled tennis shoes which later became pretty door stops.

The opportunity came for me to jump ship. The firm I worked for in Phoenix was being bought out by a bigger company. So, I decided the time was right, ready or not, I am going to start my own company with one food line. In retrospect I was really brave and crazy. But, I stuck with it, worked my tail off and survived a male-dominated business for 12 years. I finally was the boss and I was making great money. So why wasn't I happy?

I was exhausted. I didn't want to sell gourmet cake anymore. I was unhappy in my marriage. I had packed on 50 extra pounds of self-loathing. I needed help.

At 42 years old, at the peak of my Astrological mid-life crisis, I got an amazing opportunity to go to Greece. This was truly my dream trip. I would finally get to see the homeland of all the Mythological Gods and I knew they would guide me to the right path.

On the 2nd day of the trip I was in Athens and went to The Parthenon. I hugged the columns asking the Gods to talk to me. I heard nothing. On the 4th day I was walking the ancient marbled paths of Ephesus in Turkey. I knew those old stones would show me the way. I saw nothing.

On the 5th day-I went to the last place that Mary, the mother of Jesus lived.

As I tied my cloth to the fence I prayed for a miracle. On the 7th day, on the isle of Crete I was watching the sunset over the Mediterranean Sea doing a reading for myself. That's when the miracle happened, the light bulb clicked on. I am supposed to be a READER. I heard it, I saw it and most of all, I felt it. I knew that was my truth.

It all finally made sense. As a Gemini, I always have to find a healthy balance between my logical mind and my intuitive mind. Astrology worked the left half of my brain by organizing and analyzing. Tarot Cards and intuition fed the right side of my brain.

When I got back to Arizona, I enrolled in more classes and I started working part-time as a reader in an established metaphysical store. I got several opportunities to teach and I was also offered my very own Radio Show where I got to show off my skills.

Three years later I closed my food business for good and got divorced. I haven't looked back.

I now do work that I absolutely love. I call myself an Intuitive Consultant. I don't have to take orders from anyone. I work in the comfort of my home. And best of all, I can dress like a witch if I want to.

The first time people come to me, many are experiencing the same emptiness I once felt. I understand it. But I also know that we each have our own unique path to walk.

Astrology proves that to me time and time again. I have been blessed to watch many of my clients grow from a place of sadness to finding the song in their heart. Now that for me is true happiness.

Excuse me, but I need to sing now. When you wish upon a Star, makes no difference who you are, Anything your heart desires will come to you. Believe it.

Katherine Metcalf is an Intuitive Consultant. She combines her knowledge in Astrology with her intuition to help guide you on your unique path. She specializes in career counseling and business planning. Katherine does readings in the privacy of her lovely home in North Phoenix and is happy to be of service to you. She believes that you are all unique shining stars. Visit her website: www.katherinemetcalf.com.

Going For It
By Antonio Ballatore

As a kid, I wanted to be a musician. When I was sixteen, I wanted to leave school to try to pursue my music. In order to get me signed out of school, my mom made me go to work so I started working construction full time.

Construction was hard work. I started off with these guys from Texas who would work from sunup until sundown. We would do everything from masonry to roofing. I'd come home with my hands all cracked and bleeding and have to sleep with Vaseline on my hands with socks over them. It taught me how to work hard and to really push. It was pretty rough, but I was able to get my GED at night and also play my music. And it was cool every weekend to get that paycheck. Plus I could have long hair and I didn't have to worry about much.

I was making good money and working hard. I wasn't unhappy, but I knew there was something else out there for me.

My mom passed away when I was twenty years old, so I moved to the lower East side of Manhattan. I started doing a little bit of construction there, renovating clubs and bars.

Music was my life at that point. I did what I could to do my music, tour in bands and work towards trying to get a record deal. I started off playing heavy metal in the 80's and then switched over to punk rock and New York hard core. I played bass guitar. I wrote a lot of music, my favorite thing to do.

One day, I was walking down the street and ran into a friend who was working for David LaChapelle, who is this over-the-top amazing photographer who is known for all these crazy sets and blowing up stuff. He's like our generation's Andy Warhol. My friend asked if I'd like to build some stuff for them and I said, "Alright. I'll try it out."

I went in and music was cranking and people were screaming and there were drag queens running around and it was this whole crazy scene going on. I thought, "This is pretty cool."

I started building these really great sets for David LaChapelle and loved it. When I was working with David I was pushing my imagination, building whatever you could imagine. Plus it used all these skills I had from construction, and all these things I'd learned from growing up in a household with two parents who were artists. There was always a lot of art in my house and I was always pushed to be different, to do something different. Our house, growing up, had two or three different studios for painting and metal sculpture. I would help my father who was a big visual director for places like Macy's with his sets and his windows. The set design world was a whole new career for me that I really fell in love with.

Once I started working for David LaChapelle, the schedule was so intense I had to make a choice: did I want to do music or did I want to do set design? I decided to forget music and focus on set design.

That first year, I just went for it. Within four years I was landing jobs with Annie Leibovitz, Mark Seliger and all the top photographers at the time. I was living in New York. I was in a good, long-term relationship. I was cranking out some great sets, business was really great and I was big in life, man. It was pretty awesome for a while.

I've always been a stills photographer guy. I never got into doing videos, never got into doing movies or commercials. I love still photography because it's more personal, with me and the photographer coming up with concepts and doing all this crazy stuff together; and there's not a million people to go through. It's a little tighter situation, more creative.

Work was rocking but then, all of a sudden, my girlfriend and I started not getting along. We got this dog and the life I thought I had with her was just not working any more. Then 9/11 happened and we watched it from my apartment.

Right after 9/11, things in the city were a mess. Business stopped and things just started falling apart. My girlfriend and I split up after six years together. Plus I had just opened a catering business on the side with my brother and that went under.

That was one of the low points in my life. I felt really depressed and really unhappy. I was listening to a lot of like Hank Williams and country music and drinking way too much Wild Turkey.

I had been coming out to Los Angeles to work a lot, so I decided to pack up all my stuff and my dog and move to L.A. People wondered how I could leave. I had this crazy, beautiful loft; I had this woodshop; I had all these people working for me. People said, "You have all this stuff going on. How can you just let go of it and move out of New York? How can you leave your family and everybody else?"

I just had to take a chance and go for it. My dog, Chomper, a bull mastiff, and I drove out to L.A. and started fresh.

It was great in the beginning. I loved it! Work was a whole new experience because L.A. is so production-friendly, you can find so much more stuff; better props and better set-builders than in New York. It was like my career started over again. Then I had a little rough patch, but I got it back together. That was a really happy time in my life.

Since I was in L.A., I got a different agent. I started working less and less with the really crazy photographers like David LaChapelle and Annie Leibovitz and instead started doing commercial work for Proctor & Gamble and Wal-Mart and companies like that.

I was making a ton of money and really doing well financially, but creatively it was just not there. For example, my job for a week might be to search for the perfect red coffee cup. And I thought, "This isn't cool. This is not fun anymore." My love for set design started dying.

Then a friend told me about HGTV Design Star, a TV reality show in which eleven designers compete for their own show on HGTV. She said, "My friend's casting the show. You should check it out and send your picture in."

I wasn't very interested. I didn't really watch much TV. I didn't know much about it, but I thought, "Whatever, I'll just send my thing in." I made a little video and they really dug me and my stuff. I got on the show.

It was weird timing. I had been going through the motions with my work for some time. About a month before taping began, I split up with my girlfriend of the past three and half years. I thought, "Alright, I'm just going to go for it on this show."

Being a contestant on HGTV Design Star was a crazy experience. You're locked away for six weeks. There's no phone, no radio, no music. We had to work sixteen to eighteen hour days, every day, non-stop, for six weeks straight.

I never really knew what went into making a reality show. They really try to torture you to create drama, to push you against people and make you fight. In the beginning, it was super stressful. I can get worked up pretty quick and can't handle any kind of drama like they were creating.

I was ready to go home after the first two weeks. But then I realized that I could win if I just stuck it out, if I just went for it. So I did. I just went for it.

I ended up winning. Now this whole new career has started for me. People recognize me every where. I have all this crazy responsibility of being a TV show host and running a huge crew. There is a lot of pressure and some days are just unbelievable. But I love it!

I'm trying to do something different and interactive and cool with my show, The Antonio Treatment. We're having different guest artists each week. I go on these inspirational trips and meet with different people. And the crew that I brought in on my show are all my buddies. One is a friend that I grew up with; another friend I've been doing sets with for 12 or 13 years.

It's a little bit of struggle sometimes to get my vision through. People are like, "What are you thinking?" I'm like, "Just trust me. Let's just go for it." They've been pretty cool so far in letting me do what I want to do design-wise and conceptually.

You're going to see me grow as a designer. We're just getting better and better with each show. I'm excited to see people's reactions. I hope people get it. The whole thing is scary. I think that if marketed right and an appreciative crowd gets to see it, it could be super successful.

The best thing about doing my show is that I get these gigs to do whatever I dream up. There is a hotel that gave me my own suite to design. They said, "Do your own thing. We're going to call it 'The Antonio Suite'. You just do whatever you want." So I have this life-sized pink rhino coming out of the wall and a seven foot cobra headboard with laser-beams and I'm just going for it. I'm doing what I want. People ask me, "Why are you doing that?" and I say, "Why not?" I'm just being creative and being an individual and trying to do something different with design.

That's the thing: I'm really trying to be different. As a set designer, I can copy anything. Anything! Open a magazine and I can copy anybody's design or any image you see. But with this show, I'm totally trying to be myself and come up with crazy things that people either love or hate. And I get a lot of people who hate it because they're used to the cookie cutter HGTV stuff. But then I get cool people who may not want a pink rhino in their house or whatever but appreciate what I'm doing and get inspired by it.

For me, when people get inspired by what I do and then email and say, "This inspired me to paint this wall some crazy color" or whatever that makes it all worth it. That makes me feel like I'm doing something good and right. That's the best thing about all of this.

If I were to give advice to someone unhappy in their workplace, I'd say this: You only live once. Life is too short to get stuck in any position that is not fulfilling or doesn't make you happy. Life is too short! Maybe you feel trapped or that it's hard to make your move out of it, whether it's work or a relationship, but if you just make your move and go for it, you can do anything you want. Even if it doesn't pay off the way you think it should, you'll learn from the experience and be ready when the next opportunity comes along.

Happiness Awaits You!

As the winner of Season 4 of HGTV Design Star, Antonio Ballatore now hosts his own HGTV show, The Antonio Treatment. *His distinct personality and unexpected, edgy design aesthetic wows viewers. A New York native, Antonio grew up believing he would be a rock star. While pursuing his dreams of music stardom, he spent time between gigs learning how to build houses. This experience led him to design restaurants and clubs in Manhattan and, later, design sets for world-famous photographers, including Annie Leibovitz, David LaChapelle and Mark Seliger. Antonio resides in Los Angeles with his English bulldog, Chewie. Visit his website:*
http://www.hgtv.com/the-antonio-treatment/show/index.html.

The Best Receptionist in the World
By Carol Kline

When I graduated from college with a degree in literature, there wasn't a huge demand for literature grads in the marketplace. Although I wasn't sure what I wanted to do with my life, I needed to pay my rent, so I took a position as a receptionist for a busy stock brokerage firm. While the job had a lot of perks, there was one big problem: I hated being a receptionist.

Answering a phone all day was alternately stressful and boring. Within a month, I loathed getting up in the morning, and my unhappiness at work was coloring my whole life. I knew I had two choices: I could find another job or find a way to like the one I had. I decided to do both. While I looked for other employment, I searched for a way to be happier where I was.

I challenged myself to become "the best receptionist in the world." Because I'd always had a very strong sense of wanting to serve others and make a difference, I wrote the word "SERVICE" in big letters across the top of the calendar blotter on my desk.

With this reminder of my goal staring me in the face, I began answering the phone with a smile in my voice, learned to recognize frequent callers' voices and address them by name, and if it was appropriate, I'd even ask them how they were. What astounded me was how sincerely interested I was in the answer. Caring about my job had translated into caring, Period.

I'd once heard a quote from cosmetic tycoon Mary Kay Ash, "Pretend that every single person you meet has a sign around his or her neck that reads, Make Me Feel Important," and I put that concept into practice as well.

I joked around with the brokers and other staff and generally made my work day a party. Not only did my happiness level skyrocket, but within a month, I was promoted to a more interesting job within the brokerage.

Though I eventually found a way to make my living that suited me much better, I've never forgotten how I managed to turn that job –and my happiness level—around.

By Carol Kline, adapted from *Happy for No Reason: 7 Steps to Being Happier from the Inside Out*, by Marci Shimoff with Carol Kline. (Free Press, 2008)

A freelance writer/editor for over twenty-nine years, Carol Kline specializes in narrative non-fiction and self-help. With Marci Shimoff, she co-wrote the New York Times bestselling book, Happy for No Reason: 7 Steps to Being Happier from the Inside Out *and their upcoming book,* Love for No Reason. *Carol also co-authored* You've Got to Read this Book: 55 People Tell the Story of the Book that Changed Their Life *with Jack Canfield and Gay Hendricks plus* The Ultimate Cat Lover, The Ultimate Dog Lover, *as well as five books in the Chicken Soup for the Soul® series. E-mail her at: ckline@happyfornoreason.com*

The Elixir of Life
By Fahtiem

When I was a new mom, we moved to Joliet, Illinois temporarily. One day, I came across an advertisement in the local newspaper offering belly dancing classes at the local YMCA. I really didn't know much about this style of dance, but it sounded exotic. I wanted get back into shape after having my two children, so I was drawn to the idea of dancing for exercise. I loved music and was always singing around the house and dancing with the movies on TV.

I hadn't ever taken any kind of classes before, let alone dance classes. I wasn't a bold person, but I signed up anyway. More than anything, I was curious.

When I arrived, I found a group of women who were just as curious as I was. It was the first time that a belly dancing class was being offered so none of us knew what to expect.

The music started. And what music! It was classic Middle Eastern music that, although very new to me, resonated with something deep down. It made my heart sing! I felt like moving when I heard it. I had to express myself.

It felt so wonderful to move in these new and interesting ways. I loved how my body felt. Although I was insecure about how well I was executing the movements, I was truly happy. It was fun! The hour went by so fast! By the end of the class, I was so delighted I couldn't wait for the next class. The other women felt the same way. We were hooked. We did the entire eight week class and another session after that.

At the end of our second course, we had a big group performance for our family and friends. We are talking about a natural high! The experience was exhilarating, addictive and boosted my confidence tremendously, particularly when I received praise from strangers, telling me I did great.

I wanted to feel that way again and again. I realized that this dance was a way to feel good physically, mentally and spiritually. When I moved to California later that year, one of my goals was to find a teacher to continue belly dancing.

In my first class with Linda Post, I realized how much I didn't know. She'd been dancing for five years and was in a completely different world than mine. I was in awe. When she moved, everything was put together and I thought, "Wow! I want to dance like that!"I realized that I had a lot to learn.

I learned a lot from Linda and I loved learning it. It came natural to me. Even though I was shy, it was easier for me to move my hips more than some of the other women.

One of the students in Linda's class was my friend, Nancy. After about a year of lessons, we decided that we wanted to dance on a more regular basis so we went to a   restaurant and asked whether they wanted to have entertainment. They did.

Our first paying gig was very exciting. My husband did the announcing and Nancy's husband was the engineer attending to our music. We did a show. We put a turban on one of the customers in the audience and I sang. I was very shy and very scared, but I did it anyway. I made people smile, laugh and have a great time and all I had to do was have a great time myself. I was actually getting paid to do something that made me feel great and brought joy to everyone around me. They were happy and I was happy. It felt good so, I kept doing it.

Once we started, it all just started coming together. We began performing regularly at clubs and restaurants. When Nancy moved away, I kept doing it solo.

Meanwhile, a teaching position opened up at a ballroom dance studio. I really had to think about doing it. Was I ready? I was apprehensive and excited at the same time. After all, this was my first chance to share the dance I adored with others. I reflected on how much my self confidence had increased along with my understanding and skill of the dance. I was improving quickly and having fun doing it. This could be a Win! Win! I said "Yes", even though I had no idea where it would lead me. It just felt right.

My class was small at first, then the word got around. "Take belly dancing. It's fun!" My classes grew and I got referrals to teach at other places. Within a year, I was teaching at ten locations. Even today, thirty years later, I still teach six days a week.

As the years went on, I taught and performed more and more. It all unfolded so organically. I would have five or six shows a night in five or six different locations. I perfected the skill of driving and looking at maps. I did the first "Belly Grams" for a company name Gorilla Gram. I performed for the celebrations of all of life's major events: baby showers, birthdays, weddings, anniversaries, even a funeral. I even got a lot of press from the newspapers. I was in demand and felt so accomplished, doing what I loved.

In 1990, I decided to create an opportunity for people to come see the art and culture of Middle Eastern dance presented well and with respect. This was my contribution to the art form I adored: to present the best artists with the best lighting and the best sound in a big five star hotel. Oasis Dance Magic was one of the first big, beautiful well-done events. It was a top notch weekend conference with classes and a big production show. To pull it off successfully, I developed the necessary skills to become a promoter, marketing agent, booking agent, costume designer, producer and artistic director. I did this event annually for seventeen years.

It took many years before people actually labeled what I did as work. They thought that dancing and traveling was just fun. They were right, it was fun. It still is fun and it is my work. I love what I do and I love who I have become.

Middle Eastern dance has been my full time pursuit and passion over the past thirty years. It has contributed to my consistent good health. When you are happy, your body is filled with wellness hormones. Belly dancing has given me youth in a bottle. I think it's like the elixir of life!

This art form has given me many fabulous relationships and friendships. We are connected with the thread of love for the dance, the music and the happiness it brings us.

Every time I'm in the classroom, it gives me joy. Every time I'm on the stage, I'm in joy. Every time I travel and meet people, I'm in joy.

This is what I know:

> Life is a miracle, something to treasure, savor and enjoy.
> When your heart sings, you are on the right track.
> When you are filled with love everything just works.
> The opportunity for joy is available to all that are open to receive it.

Fahtiem is an award-winning choreographer, master instructor, international superstar performer, renowned in the world of Middle Eastern Dance. Featured in Time magazine, movies, commercials, TV and numerous performance and instructional DVD's, her awards include International Cultural Diploma of Honor, Woman of the Year 1991, International Academy of Middle Eastern Dance, Dancer of the Year, Entertainer of the Year, Choreographer of the Year, Teacher of the Year, American Academy of Middle Eastern Dance (New York), Hall of Fame-Lifetime Achievement, MECDA Hall of Fame and has been listed in International Who's Who of Professional and Business Women. She has co-created five musical CDs plus the instructional DVD series Bellydance Bootcamp with Fahtiem. *Visit her Website: www.fahtiem.com).*

STEPPING STONES

Our professional lives take up about a third of our work week. We owe it to ourselves, our friends, families and co-workers to be happy during this time.

If you'd like to be more joyful in your job, you have two options:

1. You can find a professional outlet for your true passions

2. You can make the best of the job you already have.

Activity: Take a moment to inventory your true passions. What do you love to do? What's as easy as breathing for you? What gave you joy as a child?

_____

_____

_____

_____

If time and money were no object, what work would you like to do?

_____

_____

_____

_____

How can you incorporate some of your answers from the above questions into your life? Are there part-time opportunities? Could you engage in them outside of work? Are there volunteer opportunities? Do you have friends who share the same interests? Could you band together to pursue them?

_____

_____

_____

_____

Activity: Explore ways to enhance your happiness at work.
How can you incorporate some of your answers from the above questions into your present job?

_____

_____

_____

_____

What elements of your present job do you enjoy the most?

_____

_____

_____

_____

What can you be grateful about in your present job?

_____

_____

_____

_____

CHAPTER 5

Was It Only a Dream?

Messages received in dreams can be prophetic or simply a reflection of the subconscious thoughts that rise to the surface during the sleep process. Dream interpretation has been going on for centuries and there are a number of books in the marketplace that offer meanings for the things that you see in your dreams. However, there are other elements that affect your dreams that must be considered along with any symbolism defined in books.

Often dreams can be traced back to things that happened during the day, television shows you watched, conversations you had with others, and factors, like heat, cold, storms, mental and emotional stress. For example, a real estate agent may dream about showing properties to difficult clients all night long. Work related dreams are simply a manifestation of the stress of the job during a busy time of year. If you go to bed hungry, your dreams may be full of images of food. Going to sleep after a scary movie, especially for children, can induce nightmares.

Many dreams are a jumble of people and things that often make no sense at all. Who are all those strangers who march around in your dreams night after night? You may never find out and that's perfectly okay. After all, dreams occur when you reach a level of deep sleep, a time when your conscious mind is at rest and not available to filter your dream images and make sense of them. Maybe that's why many dreams cannot be remembered clearly after you awake.

Nonetheless, dreams have always been expected to contain messages. Remember when girls would attend a wedding, bring a piece a wedding cake home with them and sleep with the cake under their pillow that night? The belief was that the young woman would then dream about the man she was to marry. This was a good way to smash a perfectly good piece of cake, and not a very accurate way to find a future mate.

Actors and directors will tell you that they dream about the show they are working on at night. Often the show in their dreams is a disaster, prompting them to work harder to make sure it's a success.

All that aside, there are dreams that do make sense and those are the ones you should pay attention to because they can help you in your daily life. There are messages that you receive in your sleep that are important to you mentally and emotionally.

One of the most common of these dreams is when you dream about deceased friends and relatives. Sometimes that is just a way the subconscious mind helps you keep memories of those loved ones close, but sometimes the dream has a more significant purpose. Consider a woman with a good friend who decided to stop taking dialysis and let her kidneys fail. The woman became very angry with her friend for doing that feeling that her friend was being inconsiderate and selfish by choosing to die rather than to keep fighting for her life.

The woman carried this anger for her friend around for months after the friend's funeral. Then, one night she had a dream. She saw her friend sitting at a picnic table in a lovely wooded area. There were other people the woman did not know sitting with her friend who was laughing and having a wonderful time. When the woman awoke, the anger she had felt at her friend was gone. Her dream helped her realize that her friend had found a freedom and happiness on the other side that she would not have been able to experience with her illness.

Over the years, you may also dream about certain images or symbols that come to have a special meaning for you. For instance, dreaming about flowers that are bright and beautiful can mean something good is about to happen in your life, while dreaming of wilted dead flowers may mean that trouble is on the way.

Although dreaming about images that mean something to you can be prophetic, they are not actually what one would call a psychic dream. As stated earlier, the conscious mind is usually asleep along with your body when you are dreaming. Most psychic dreams occur just as you are waking up and your conscious mind is coming to attention. When a dream is psychic, you instantly come awake and are fully aware of what the dream was about. The other thing that tells you the dream may come true is that the image it sent to you cannot be easily dismissed. Images in psychic dreams stay with you.

Why do people have psychic dreams? It is believed that people who experience psychic dreams are especially intuitive, but are too busy and distracted with other things during their waking hours to allow messages to get through to them. The only time the messages are allowed to surface is at night when their bodies are at rest. Having psychic dreams can be unnerving but they stem from the power of the universe that is inside all of us. They are one of the many ways that connect us to one another in love and harmony.

Psychic Dreams
By Carol Costa

Perhaps the best way to explain psychic dreams is to begin with the one that changed my life. This was probably not the first psychic dream I ever had, but it was the first one that involved a serious situation. It was the one that made me realize that people in my life were connected to me by a bond that transcended time and space.

In the dream, I saw my friend, Judy, standing with her two children and crying. I asked her what was wrong. She said, "Bill is gone." I awoke with a start.

As my busy morning moved forward, I told myself it was just a dream and tried to banish the disturbing images from my mind, but I couldn't shake the feeling of foreboding. Finally, I decided to call Judy and put my fears to rest. As I reached for the phone, it rang. The caller was Judy.

"Are you sitting down?" Judy asked in a calm voice.

"No," I replied.

"Then find a seat," she said. "I have something to tell you."

I honestly thought she was going to say that Bill was dead. Instead she told me that Bill had come home from a business trip that morning and asked her for a divorce. He admitted to having an affair and wanted to be free to marry his mistress.

I couldn't have been more shocked if my own husband had been the one making such a request. Everyone who knew Bill thought he was a great guy, the type of husband that wives told their spouses to imitate. The idea that Bill would take up with another woman and dump his wife and kids was unthinkable, yet somehow the possibility had found its way into my dream.

I didn't tell Judy about the premonition of trouble I'd had in my sleep. The last thing she needed to hear from me was that I had dreamed about her marriage falling apart.

In the weeks that followed, I concentrated on being supportive to my friend who was shattered by her husband's unfaithfulness and his disregard for her and their two young sons.

At the same time, I was doing a pretty good job of convincing myself that my dream was just a fluke, something that would never happen again, when it did happen again.

Different people, different circumstances but the same result; the dream came true.

I didn't want to have these dreams. I didn't want to know that something was going to happen before it actually occurred. I did want to know how it was possible and why it was suddenly happening to me. Up to this point in my life, I had no interest in the supernatural. I wasn't a skeptic or a non-believer; I just never gave it any thought at all.

Now I understand that the dreams were a catalyst that sent me on a life-changing journey to research the world of psychic phenomena and all things metaphysical.

The journey soon became a spiritual awakening, a new awareness of life and love. I explored the psychic links that allow us to communicate with those who have crossed over. I found pathways that led to peace, understanding, comfort and knowledge.

I have learned to embrace the dream images that I receive. Although those first dreams were disturbing, many of the others I've had over the years have contained good news, funny happenings, and messages that have helped me remember my place and purpose in the universe.

Carol Costa is a co-author of this book.

More Than a Dream
By Neva Howell

As sort of an etheric alchemist by nature, I've worked with my dreams in a spiritual way for most of my adult life. I could write a book about all the dreams I've had that were more than a dream. Three examples come to mind that were potent proof we are all connected and that, in dreamtime, we can communicate with people or animals.

I dreamed of a woman with long, straight dark hair. Her hair was parted in the middle and she had bangs. I saw her face very clearly. She played a guitar and was singing a song I also heard clearly. When I awoke, I knew that I was supposed to write down the words to the song and to remember the tune.

The next night, a friend of ours visited from Nashville. A friend made the trip with her, someone I had never met. After I hugged my friend and looked behind her, I saw the woman in my dream walking toward me. As I hugged her (I have always been big on hugs, even with strangers) and without even thinking of how it might sound, I whispered in her ear "You were in my dreams last night". Heaven only knows what she must have thought about the impulsive statement.

Later that night, I shared my dream with her. She was quiet and had a funny look on her face. I learned she played guitar and, indeed, had her guitar in my friend's car. She brought her guitar in, I taught her the song I had heard and she ended up recording it.

That wasn't the first time I dreamed of someone I had never met and then met the person from my dream. I was in Lawrenceburg, Indiana where I had reserved a booth at a holistic fair the next day and was staying with friends overnight. In my dream, a muscular man was walking toward me when he fell in a hole. As I went to help him out of the hole, he kept turning into a deer and then back into a man. When he was the deer, he looked afraid. When he was the man, he assumed a martial arts stance and appeared

100

ready to attack me if I came any closer. We had this stand-off for some time and then I woke up.

The next day, after setting up my booth and getting ready to start accepting people for healing facilitation work, I saw the man I had dreamed about walk into the building. I went straight up to him and, like the woman with the guitar, I said "You were in my dreams last night." His girlfriend standing next to him did not seem amused.

I found out that he was a martial arts instructor. When I told him the dream, he shared with me that he felt a struggle within himself that he could never be gentle and trusting like the deer. Much later, this gentle warrior got attuned to Reiki and embraced his gentle aspects in a powerful way that helps others.

The third dream which was more than a dream involved my dog. I was outside, up the side of the big hill across the road from our house. I was standing by a very big rock and there was a large plantain plant on it. In the dream I knew this was odd because plantain doesn't grow on rocks. Next to the rock was my dog. She lifted her head up and turned her neck toward me. I could see that she had cut her neck somehow. The dream was so real that it woke me up. I felt as if I had actually been outside, in the cold, looking at the cut on the dog's neck.

The next morning, I went outside to feed the animals and there the dog sat, just as she had sat patiently in my dream. As I walked toward her, she lifted her head and turned her head, just as she had done in the dream. There was the same cut I had seen.

I knew instantly that I needed to get some of my first aid salve, which contained a lot of plantain, and apply it to the cut. Not only did the dream tell me the dog was injured but it gave me the correct first aid to use!

Happiness Awaits You!

Neva Howell enjoys visionary writing and painting, the metaphysical aspects of the performing arts, and the exploration of etheric alchemy. Neva has been a spiritual healing facilitator, assisting others in positively shifting their lives since 1991. She is a professional actress and teaches an acting technique based on metaphysical principles called, The Power Connection. *In addition, Neva is a visionary artist and creates etheric alchemy watercolors and acrylics. Visit her website: http://www. askahealer.com and her Blog: http://healthychoices.askahealer. com*

The Dog of My Dreams
By Carol Costa

It had been a really bad week. An argument with my best friend, a meeting in the principal's office concerning my youngest son's bad behavior, a bill for an unexpected home repair, and the fact that I was a staff accountant at a CPA firm and it was tax season had me wishing I could run away and hide until my four children passed through puberty and became adults.

I fell into bed that Friday night and willed my mind to stop replaying the problems of the week. Finally I fell asleep only to dream that I was at the office interviewing tax clients who had showed up with their records stuffed in paper bags and shoeboxes. Then, as it happens in dreams I found myself sitting next to a pilot in a small airplane. That was probably my desire to fly away resurfacing, but the dream continued with the sudden appearance of a little white dog that jumped into my lap.

At first I tried to push the dog away, but he refused to budge, nestling his furry body against mine and licking my hands. He was so sweet and loving I gave in and cuddled him until I awoke and found it was morning again. The little dog stayed in my thoughts for the entire day. I took my canine buddy's appearance in my dream as a sign that things were going to get better, and they did.

A week or so later, a woman I worked with told me that she had found a lost miniature poodle. She had put ads in the paper, but no one had claimed him so she asked if I would consider taking him. She assured me that he had all the qualities I wanted in a pet. He didn't shed and was house-broken and well-behaved. Since my kids had been asking for a dog for a long time, I told her I would take him.

The kids were really excited about getting a dog, but just as we were about to leave the house, the phone rang. It was my co-worker. "I'm so sorry but the dog's owner just showed up on my doorstep and claimed the poodle."

I hung up and delivered the bad news to my children. My youngest daughter began to cry while her older siblings protested the unfairness of the situation.

"Okay," I said half-heartedly. "I promised you a dog and we will get a dog."

"Let's go to the Humane Society," one of them suggested. "They have lots of dogs that need a good home. We can still get one today."

"All right," I said. "But it has to be a dog that is house-broken and doesn't shed. And the dog will not be allowed on the furniture."

With the rules set, we piled into the car and headed for the Humane Society. They did indeed have lots of dogs that barked and whined as the kids ran up and down among the kennels looking for a pet. I lagged behind, wishing I had never agreed to take the lost poodle.

My boys were standing in front of a kennel containing a huge, hairy beast of undetermined breeding. I hurried towards them intending to issue a veto, when they lost interest in that dog and moved on. I stopped in my tracks.

It was then that I glanced into the kennel I had ended up in front of and saw him. I was so stunned I couldn't move, but the little white dog dashed forward to greet me. Despite his small size he was so happy to see me, he jumped five feet in the air and barked at me.

It was the dog from my dream and for some reason the realization caused me to burst into tears. "Come and look at this dog," I called to my kids.

"He's a terrier," my oldest daughter informed me. "He'll shed and little dogs always want to be on the furniture."

"This is the dog we're adopting," I announced, ignoring her warning. "His name is Casey."

"How do you know that?" my son asked.

I didn't know how I knew his name. I just did. When we filled out the papers to adopt Casey I learned that he had been brought in as a stray the same day I had dreamed about him.

"He's a Cairn Terrier and small dogs like this usually go really fast," the clerk told me. "I was surprised when I came to work this morning and he was still here."

"He was waiting for me," I told her.

Over the years, I've had many dreams of a prophetic nature, but none have predicted the happiness and fun that Casey brought into our home. He was part of our family for the next ten years and was the best, most loving dog you could imagine.

Of course my daughter had been right when she said he'd shed and get on the furniture, but I didn't care at all.

Carol Costa is a co-author of this book.

The Brady Bunch Luau
By Julie Murphy Casserly

As a financial wellness expert, I've counseled thousands of people who believe that if only they had enough money, they'd finally feel content. People always think money will make them happy, but it doesn't. What makes us happy is when we pursue our true dreams and desires, when we follow the messages our authentic selves are always trying to tell us.

When I counsel people, I coach them in terms of the different realms of their life: financial, personal, family, work and spiritual. Imagine your life is structured like a solar system with these elements orbiting around you and in the center is the source of your passion and purpose. This creates a powerful force at the center of your world, a gravity that keeps all other aspects circling it in an emotional and spiritual orbit.

Many of us place the financial realm in the middle, giving it the power to influence all the other aspects of our lives. But if instead you place your spiritual realm, what I call Inner Wealth, at the center of your life, the other aspects of your life will shift and you will create real happiness. Inner Wealth is the part of you that contains your conscience, values and core beliefs. It's also the source of your dreams, your desires, your individuality and your life's purpose.

When you're ready to place your Inner Wealth at the center of your life, you're ready to heal your relationship with money and you're ready to be happy. That's the only way to create long-term, positive change.

When you place something other than your Inner Wealth at the center of your life, you create patterns of financial difficulties. For example, you may recreate a debt cycle or find yourself repeatedly sabotaging your business. You may find yourself in a job you don't like and feel that you can't leave because you're so deep in debt. America is in its current financial state because we forgot to follow our dreams as opposed to trying to find happiness from the outside in versus the inside out.

When we're deep in financial trouble, we can't even fathom shifting our behavior or changing what we've put in the center of our lives. But that's exactly what we need to do to restore our financial situation and to find true contentment. The irony is that our authentic self is always trying to tell us what to do to make things better. It sends us messages in different ways: through words or symbols or visual pictures. Often, it sends us images through our dreams.

And those messages repeat: when you start to see things come to you more than once, that's when you've got to really start paying attention. For example, maybe you keep attracting 'takers' as friends. They have different faces and different names but each of them is hurting you with the same 'gimme gimme gimme' behavior. When you detect a pattern, you can look for the message. For example: "These people are taking advantage of my giving nature. I must set new boundaries."

Yet, for the most part, we dismiss these messages. We ignore them. For whatever reason, we don't shift and move until there's a strong enough compelling reason, whatever that is.

I have a client who was a senior manager in an accounting firm she had been with for fifteen years. She came to me and said, "I can't believe I was laid off!" I said, "Really? You've hated being there for at least six years but for whatever reason you couldn't unplug yourself even though you dreamed of being an entrepreneur. You know the signs were there along the way, but for whatever reason you couldn't muster up the courage to unplug there and plug in somewhere else."

I've seen this pattern happen over and over again. If you're not willing to move and shift then eventually the universe and God will do it for you. Early on, she probably didn't see the signs. In more recent years, she did see opportunities being provided to get her closer and closer to her dream of being an entrepreneur, but she would never pull the trigger. I even suggested she test-pilot her dream by working for a smaller company so she could get the feel of what it felt like; start to wear it a little bit, like a coat. This would have allowed her to activate more and more of her true dream and desire, but she didn't do it.

When you don't follow your dreams, you may start to financially act out with credit card debt or through abuse in other areas. In her case, she had huge credit card debt at one point, that she paid down then built back up before paying it back down again. Meanwhile, she was carrying around seventy extra pounds on her body.

As humans, we do much better in collaboration with other human beings. Yet she would always alienate people in her life. And the more she would alienate them, the more she would incur debt or gain weight. Things got worse over the years; still she couldn't make a shift. She waited and waited until her company laid her off.

This woman has been unemployed for months and she's still stuck. I keep asking her, "Why are you not starting that dream company you've always talked about?" She knows she should be, but for whatever reason, she's not following her dreams.

There's something in her subconscious holding her back. She's not receiving the messages her authentic self is sending her. I've had the same thing happen to me. There was something in my subconscious that was holding me back from the career success to which I aspired.

My dream was to financially heal America, and then to have an impact globally. I know what I do helps people regain their personal power from money and start to live high quality lives. I've been doing it one-on-one, and now I'm doing speaking engagements that continue to get larger and larger.

Before I started down the path I was meant to follow, I kept having this recurring dream that helped me figure out what my authentic self was trying to tell me. Did you ever see that old Brady Bunch episode where they went to Hawaii? At one point they were at a luau. In my recurring dream, I was there at the Brady Bunch luau with my eleven brothers and sisters and the rest of my family. Then, all of a sudden, one by one, the people I cared about were disappearing. I kept calling, "Where are you? Where did you guys go?"

I kept having this dream over and over again. In some of the work I did with one of my healers, we noted that in my family of twelve children, we've always been a pack. We do things for each other. No one was supposed to break out from the pack. My subconscious fear was that if I succeeded in my career, then my family wouldn't be able to identify with me anymore. They wouldn't know me and I would lose them. I was going to be left all by myself up at the top. Once I identified that fear, I had to heal it internally. And when I did my healing work, my career blossomed.

Of course my fears were completely unfounded. As I get more and more successful, my family members are my biggest cheerleaders. They're just tickled pink, proud to be my family! And I'm certainly not alone. Everyone laughs because almost everyone who works for me is related to me in some fashion. The pack is supporting me rather than abandoning me.

If you're not happy, if you're not content with your financial situation, scan your environment for messages you might be missing. What patterns are reoccurring? What are your dreams telling you? Your authentic self is trying to help you, if only you will listen.

Julie Murphy Casserly, CLU, ChFC, CFP®, is a 15-year veteran of the financial services industry and author of the award-winning book, The Emotion Behind Money: Building Wealth from the Inside Out. *A Chicago-based entrepreneur, Julie founded JMC Wealth in 2000 and now works with more than 2,500 clients worldwide on all aspects of their financial portfolio's including investment asset allocation, risk management, insurance needs, retirement planning, business planning, college planning and estate planning. A graduate of the University of Illinois-Urbana/ Champaign, Julie earned an MBA from The University of Notre Dame. Visit her website: www.emotionbehindmoney.com*

Saying Good-Bye
By Carol Costa

I believe that some people you encounter during your life are sent to you as examples of how you should behave and how you should treat others. Mark was one of those amazing people who never had a bad word to say about anyone. He treasured his family and his many friendships. Although I had known Mark since he was a high school student, his incredible compassion and generosity didn't really become known to me until many years later when we worked together for the charity organization at our parish church that helped the poor in our community.

I was the treasurer and Mark had just been elected president which meant that he and I had to work closely together. Mark was self-employed as a coin dealer and often he would come to my house to give me a cash donation for our organization. When I would ask who I should send a receipt or a thank you letter to he would just say the donor wanted to remain anonymous. I soon realized that Mark was the donor and anytime he made extra money in his business dealings, he would donate the money to the charity group that he already spent countless hours helping.

When Mark suffered a serious heart attack when he was in his early forties, everyone who knew him prayed for his recovery. He did recover and as soon as he was able went back to work for our charity group. Although he was no longer the president he still showed up at my door on a regular basis with cash donations for me to add to the organization's treasury.

The day before Mark and his mother were to travel across the country to visit his younger brother and his brother's family, he stopped at my house and handed me a thousand dollars in cash. This time he said it was a donation from an uncle who lived in Texas. I later found out that it was actually payment Mark had received for a coin purchase the uncle had made.

About ten days into Mark's trip I received a phone call that Mark had suffered another heart attack and was in intensive care in a hospital near his brother's home. Once again everyone began praying for Mark's recovery. None of the members of our charity group could imagine how we would get along without Mark to work along side of us.

"God let us keep him last time," people said. "He must know how much we still need him."

That night, I dreamed that I was outside at some type of gathering and I saw Mark making his way through the crowd towards me. He was dressed in jeans and a t-shirt, the clothes he always wore when sorting food for the poor, delivering beds to those who had none, and just generally offering a helping hand to anyone in need. Only this time instead of his customary blue denim outfit, Mark's clothes were dazzling white.

In the dream, I stood waiting for him to reach me and when he did he gave me a great big hug. Then, he smiled, turned and walked away. The next morning I learned that Mark had passed away the night before.

Some say that dreams are powerful tools that help us cope with life. I agree that they are. However, I also say dreams are prophetic and the way people we love sometimes say good-bye.

Carol Costa is a co-author of this book.

STEPPING STONES

The thing to remember about dreams is that they are filtered through your subconscious mind. Since your subconscious mind is like a tape recorder that captures everything that is going on your life, it is wise to examine recent happenings in your life to see if they may have influenced your dreams.

When you have elements in your dreams that disturb you, write them down and then think about the current happenings in your life. Can you find a way to overcome these challenges and turn them into opportunities for growth.

_____

_____

_____

_____

If you want to stop dreaming about these images, put your conscious mind to work and list positive qualities about people, places, or things that you find unsettling. This will help you change your feelings about them. Also see the chapter, The Power of Forgiveness, for further help.

_____

_____

_____

_____

Before falling asleep at night, try to clear your mind of problems. Say a prayer of thanksgiving for any good things or people that touched your life that day.
Take deep breaths and when you exhale imagine that all the day's problems and worries are being blown away from you.

Remember that dreams often contain messages and ideas but they are also fleeting images and may fade with the morning light. Take the time to write down what you want to retain as soon as you awake from the dream.

_____

_____

_____

_____

Pay particular attention to dream images that reoccur and determine whether they alert you to challenges or impending good fortune.

If you consult a dream book or other guide to interpret your dreams, remember that the way you feel about the dream is the most important thing. Don't be misled by definitions that conflict with your feelings.

CHAPTER 6

Blessings in Disguise

Sometimes, bad things happen. But are they truly 'bad'? In the heat of the moment, it's very difficult to be accurate in assessing how 'bad' or 'good' something is. We are apt to get swept up in the drama of the event. We get pulled into the details and emotions of the moment. It's difficult to take a step back and consider that this noxious incident has any silver lining. But often, a challenging event leads to something better.

Jerzy Kosinski, award-winning author of novels such as *Being There*, is a case in point. As a Jewish child growing up in Poland during World War II, he lived through difficult times, indeed. Many would squelch this kind of past, but Jerzy Kosinski wove his experiences into a highly acclaimed novel *The Painted Bird*. The book launched Kosinski's stellar writing career and provided new, vivid insight into the abuses of the World War era, a salve and gift for many.

What if the seemingly bad events in our lives are there to bring our attention to something that we need to change or face? Or maybe there is something to learn from this unwanted event that will accelerate our spiritual growth.

Consider how to find joy and happiness from unexpected circumstances. Perhaps an illness may give you much needed time to reflect on what truly matters. Time is precious, and often we don't take time for ourselves.

Getting fired is never pleasant, but if it's really providing a course correction that leads a person to a job for which they are better suited, it could be their best career move ever.

Some people are losing their homes due to recent economic situations. But maybe downsizing can be freeing. Maybe it is time to shed possessions that no longer serve our highest good? Such an event, even when unplanned, can assist us in valuing what is really important in life versus the material processions that we may cling to.

They say that first something may seem like an obstacle to us, then it becomes a challenge, and finally it becomes a blessing. This chapter shows examples of how obstacles and challenges have been turned into Blessings in Disguise

Faith and the Power of the Mind
By D. H. Palmer

I can still remember hearing the voices. Men were talking about me as if I were not there. As I listened I became aware that I was in an emergency room. The doctors busily stitching me up assumed I was still unconscious and freely discussed what they were doing to the various parts of my anatomy.

The tugging I felt on my scalp area was a doctor putting the equivalent of two feet of stitches in my head. Another doctor was sewing up multiple lacerations on my right arm around the wrist and over the elbow. The third doctor was doing work around my left eye. It was his comments that stayed with me the most over all these years. He said, "When I am done with stitching her up, this will be so fine a line that as she ages it will seem like just one of her laugh lines."

He seemed to be of the opinion that I'd be around for a very long time so he was going to make sure I looked good for the journey. I later learned he was a plastic surgeon. He did an amazing job considering the line he was discussing was from the center of the lid on my left eye three inches down my face toward my cheekbone.

How did I end up listening to voices in an emergency room? I was a passenger in my girlfriend's car traveling down the number five freeway near La Jolla, California. In a distracted moment, we were in an accident witnesses said flipped the car end over end two times and then rolled side over side five times.

The doctors I encountered on my long odyssey of recovery were less optimistic than the plastic surgeon in the emergency room. I delved deep into my soul using an invisible and intangible faith to find the strength to heal; a three year battle to get the me I knew I was meant to be back.

I was bandaged from the top of my head to my tailbone and on my right leg and right arm when they released me from the hospital. It was not until I was able to remove some of the bandages and see other doctors that I had a true sense of the damage inflicted on my body. A hole the size of a quarter had been stitched up near my right knee. Whatever had punctured the area also affected the meniscus so severely, every doctor I consulted said I would never be able to walk normally again. Prior to the accident I ran five to eight miles a day and truly enjoyed the runner's high. I was told I would never be able to run again.

My rotator cuff on my right shoulder had been so damaged I was told I would never be able to raise my right arm any higher than the height of my waist.

I also had a broken finger on my right hand. After a year of constant therapy to regain the use of my right arm, a very good hand surgeon sawed a bone in my hand and rotated it to reposition my index finger, enabling me to regain more normal function of the finger.

The recovery from the surgery and the therapy taught me that one can endure an incredible amount of pain. I learned that morphine wears off, and after awhile I figured out natural remedies to help me deal with the constant unrelenting agony as my bones, muscles, and ligaments healed.

One specialist after another repeatedly told me I would never walk normally again. They went so far as to say my life would be filled with many 'never again' limitations. The list was long and heartbreaking.

I decided not to let the doom and gloom prediction of the doctors be a part of my consciousness. Each time I shut out their words and replaced them with thoughts of wellness and healing. I refused to even go there with any part of my being. In my head, I wrote the final outcome I wanted; a visual image of health and wholeness.

The loved ones in my life, friends and family, helped me and supported me the best they could, but they were not coming from the same faith-based strength. My journey, except for self-help books and my own determination, was indeed a solo one.

I have always believed the mind speaks to the body and soul; that we must listen and believe in this truth. This horrific accident was going to be proof to myself, that this amazing power of the mind can conquer all. With the determination and discipline I knew I could muster, I was going to make everyone of those expert doctors wrong!

Brave and powerful words, but I was surrounded by negativity and few words of encouragement. Those who loved me would parrot the words of the experts. I found myself in a sea of people who meant well but did not accept our ability to draw on the power of our god self energy to heal ourselves. I knew I was traveling a road not often taken.

I didn't want to do the journey alone. It made me sad to think of this as a solo trip. As I became more determined, I became stronger. I realized I am never alone because the god force is always with me. I related this awareness to the soul's journey to joy and wisdom with the universal god force, also a solo trip. We can go to church, meditate, etc. but ultimately the intimate contact we each have with our concept of God is an individual one, a solo one, a blessed sacred holy union between self and god self.

Even now, I consciously monitor my thoughts. I understood through first-hand experience the power of the mind; an amazing force which can be used to destroy or create. I chose creation and co-creating with the God energy within. Each day I told all the cells in my body they were getting better and better, and they listened.

I finally got it. I am capable, to dream, believe and achieve all that I set out to do. Having faith in myself is where my strength emanates from. It is the power of the mind which creates the reality we find ourselves in, and I am determined to create a beautiful and joyous world for myself.

D.H. Palmer's bio follows her story in Chapter 2.

Evolving the Family Life
By Mark Mansfield

From the moment I heard, I knew my child would be a boy. The men in my father's line, going back at least two generations, maybe more, were not emotionally demonstrative. There was love underneath, expressed in gestures, but they were the stoic providers. Presence was often absent and emotional connections were rare. Not through any intentional distancing, but rather because they never learned how. I was determined that I was going to be a different, more present father. I was determined to evolve the family line.

As often happens, the healing came in layers. When Izaac was five months old, we moved from Arizona to Michigan for more family support and contact. For the next year we lived with my parents. It was the first time I had lived with them in almost ten years. Funny how quickly the old wounds begin to ache.

Although old patterns were triggered from time to time, as an adult I was able to step outside of the old roles. I was often able to see our relationship from a higher perspective. There were still those things that pushed my buttons, like feeling my father didn't value my perspective. This put me face to face with the key ways I was going to be different. Holding my baby, who was just beginning to crawl, I reflected on how my relationship with my dad has affected many areas of my life and promised my son different, more empowered experiences.

In the midst of my pain tapes I noticed something else. My dad had grown. He was not the same man I knew as a child. Sure, there were some old habits, but he had learned; he was trying. The combination of looking at old resentments with new eyes and seeing new things in old people allowed me to release the pain, and therefore the patterns, around the father-son relationship, preparing me for the next stage.

Finally able to afford to move, my wife and I bought a house close to my parents and set about making it our own. We painted, repaired, parented, and dreamed. I felt like I had arrived at some kind of way station to adulthood. More importantly, after the brief detour with my old family, I felt better prepared than ever to pave a smoother road with my new family.

Izaac was two and beginning to explore and develop personality. With personality comes a deeper level of relationship, and I tried my best to be the kind of dad I always wanted for myself: attentive, demonstrative, supportive. I think in many ways I succeeded, but looking back there were definitely areas where I fell short. My patience and temper were short at times, like my dad and granddad. Though I tried to be conscious, there were times I found myself waking up at the other end of a pattern with nothing I could do but damage control. It helped to remember that my dad had changed.

Despite the automatic reactions, I noticed areas where I had evolved the family line. I was more present and emotionally available, as well as more open to and supportive of my child's uniqueness. I complimented him whenever possible, and made sure I was aware of developmental issues that might arise. In short, I kept a conscious desire to do things differently and was therefore more aware in our day-to-day interactions.

It was the best six months of living the dream that I could create. Relationship, however, is a co-creation and underneath this illusion was seething the seed of separation. My wife decided that she did not share this particular dream and so we separated.

Towards the end there was the fighting and yelling, the blaming, the hurting. When I was able to take a step back and look objectively at the situation, I grieved for Izaac and the experiences he was having as a result of his parent's dramas. In between, I became a master of denial. My happy family was going to continue, this was just a bump in the road. It was this attitude that caused me to fall flat on my face when the divorce papers were finalized.

I truly believe we are never given more than we can handle, though at times I felt like I was on my knees. I understand now that these experiences are like high-impact field tests to shake out imperfections so they can be examined and improved. More than that, high stress situations push us into operating from our automatic programming so we can hopefully examine and modify it.

Funny, single dad was the last title I would have considered for myself, but it turns out to have been the best. Living together while separated was intended to lessen the impact of imminent change. Though it caused more pain, I am grateful for that difficult time and the opportunities it presented to become conscious of my automatic responses and true desires for my family.

I am grateful for my situation as I realize that there are those struggling a lot more than I am. My ex-wife and I get along better now than we did when we were married. We live close enough to each have Izaac half the week. We are supportive of each other's lives and have our son's needs as the number one priority.

When I was forced to look outside what I thought it meant to be a father and a family, I found something different than I was expecting, but better suited to the unique entities comprising this family. Though I occasionally feel sad that my son is not with me full time, I am generally grateful for the freedom allowed by the part time status. I try to get all of my errands and tasks out of the way when I am alone so when we are together I can focus on having fun. Because my time with him is short, I am more present when we are together. I am, in short, more of the father I needed to be to break the chain that I knew, from the beginning, needed breaking.

Maybe you can relate to my particular situation, or maybe your painful experience encompasses another area of your life. The reality is we can all experience deeply transformative self-realization out of what we might consider, on the surface, a negative experience.

It's not always easy to maintain a positive attitude in the face of adversity. But I offer you three lessons which I hope will make it easier. First, consider that a pearl is created within an oyster from the irritation of a single grain of sand. Little did I know from out of the pain would emerge something infinitely better than I could have imagined with my small mind. Second, know that all experiences, good and bad, joyful and painful, are gifts given to us for the purposes of growth. Finally, remember that change is constant. It may feel like you are at the end of your rope right now, but the tide will shift and you will return stronger and wiser, retooled and better able to handle whatever comes next.

Mark Mansfield is a writer who has spent the last decade as a Masters Level Counselor working with kids and individuals with special needs. He also does music reviews and can be reached by e-mailing: poetryman1972@yahoo.com

The Path to Happiness
By Denise K. Davis

The first time change really rocked my world I was in my late twenties. It took me totally by surprise and left me feeling confused and at a loss about what to do. I didn't have any tools to deal with my situation. I felt frustrated that I couldn't control the circumstances, and I felt inadequate. Within a month, however, a new development presented itself that was not only better, but absolutely perfect for me.

I realized from the experience that change didn't have to be a bad thing. Was it possible that any seemingly awful situation would result in something better?

Many years have passed since then and I've endured harder changes and far tougher challenges. I realized that how we face changes and challenges determines whether they are positive or negative for us. The answer to the above question is "Yes," but how do we get through hard times until the positive reveals itself? How do we find happiness when we're faced with a devastating loss or illness? How do we get through a financial crisis? I have faced all of these at one time or another in my life. I want to share some of the beliefs and strategies that have helped me not only get through these hard times, but to achieve happiness as well.

Eight years ago, my life was terrific. I had a wonderful job, a great salary, and the best relationship I'd ever had. I had struggled most of my life with being overweight, but had finally achieved a healthy, wonderful body. Life was great and I was happy. Then the love of my life left me. I was devastated. I couldn't imagine how such a wonderful love didn't work out.

I had had enough experience by now to know that every change brings something better. Yet I found myself stuck, wanting that person back. I was very depressed. The luster of life was gone for me and I struggled to get through the days. Shortly after, I lost my job and couldn't find another. Not only was I still reeling from my love life, now I was in financial straights. There was the emotional loss of colleagues and relationships and the opportunity to do something that was incredibly fulfilling. I went through my savings and borrowed from relatives but still couldn't find a job. As I found myself alone and very lonely, and struggling to keep my home, happiness seemed far, far away.

I fell into the trap of thinking that if only I'd fall in love again I'd be all right. I'd be happy. If only I could get a job, I'd be happy. Everything would be okay again. If only certain things would happen to me, I'd be happy. I felt controlled by my circumstances. I couldn't imagine how to be happy. How can you be happy when you are not happy? I was cranky about my life; unhappy and cranky. When life's circumstances didn't rescue me, I decided I had to do something. I had to go back to what I knew. I had to get out of my funk and change my life. I couldn't spend one more minute being so unhappy.

I went back to reading spiritual literature. I was reminded of several things I'd learned over the years. First, happiness comes from within, not from any particular person or circumstance. Second, you can't control the world around you or what other people do. Third, you can control you and how you choose to experience and define what happens to you. (This is what is meant by creating your own reality.) Fourth, you have to do it yourself. Friends and family can support and love you, but you are the only one who can change you. And last, you need faith. Faith is the companion, the guide, the strength to see you through. Faith is the path to happiness.

Faith is belief. It's belief in God or some higher presence, force, or entity. The name doesn't matter. What matters is that you believe in some greater force that is personal, who loves you, and who is only interested in your happiness. This Presence is your guide. God promises you that you can have happiness and God will show you how.

Along with faith in God, you have to believe in yourself. You have to believe you are worthy. You are worthy of happiness. It helps if you believe you have a higher, more knowing consciousness always present to guide you. This consciousness is your divine connection to God.

The goal is to find happiness, no matter what. It involves divorcing yourself from the outer world and embracing the inner Truth of your wonderfulness. It involves welcoming life's experiences regardless of what they are. I believe that it's possible for such a transition to happen instantly. I've read of instances where this has happened and I confess that early on I was looking for a bolt of lightening to strike me and in a split second make me whole. However, that wasn't my path. And that was another lesson.

I realized I was still looking for something outside myself to do the work for me. Instead I had to do it in my own time. Darn! That's where faith played such an important role. Faith kept me steadfast in my belief that I could make the shift to look within, to stop trying to control the world around me and to find true happiness.

Part of faith involves accessing your Higher Self and communicating with God, but how do we do that? How do we communicate with this amorphous entity? I began consciously asking and watching. I found answers to every question I asked. I found them in animal cards, in the appearance of feathers, in song lyrics, in the utterance of a stranger, in books and movies and in communications. So will you. You'll find them in whatever ways reflect your beliefs and interests. Direction can come from your inner voice, or through a persistent thought that tells you something. Don't ignore the messages! When an answer comes, you'll know it. You'll feel a rush of truth in your heart. You'll feel a sense of knowing throughout your being.

My guidance urged me to have faith that these situations were temporary and leading to something wonderful. It also encouraged me to stop focusing on them, and instead to focus on being grateful and peaceful each moment. Faith is what gets you through the dark times, when something better is not in sight. It reminds me of the expression, when God closes a door, He opens a window, but in the meantime, you're in a dark hallway. Faith holds your hand in the darkness. It reminds you that you are not alone. It supports you through the pain and the fear and the confusion. I was reminded to be grateful for everything I have, for all the kinds of love in my life, for all the many kinds of abundance I have right now, for my health and for being alive. I worked daily to look within, have faith, and enjoy what each day brought.

Before I could do that, I felt like I needed to sort out my feelings. To help me, I used a journal. I honestly wrote everything I felt about love and my lover and my past loves. I wrote about the anger, the hurt, the expectations, and the disappointments. Then I looked for patterns in me I might want to change. I decided to stop feeling so lost and victimized. I decided to learn more about myself and how I was in relationships. I wrote about how it felt to be without a job and worried about how to pay bills. Then I shifted my thinking to my faith that I would be taken care of. I decided to look for the good in what happened.

I also used affirmations to change how I thought about things. Affirmations are simply positive statements that reflect your beliefs. I used statements like: "I deserve to be happy.", "My life is full of joy.", "The perfect job is coming my way.", "I have infinite abundance.", and "My life is full of love." I started to feel differently about my circumstances and myself.

Taking control of my life was a wonderful feeling. To realize that I had the power to decide how I was going to experience the events and conditions of my life was an amazing, uplifting feeling. I began by redefining conditions of my happiness. I stopped looking to other people or situations to make me happy. I stopped feeling sorry for myself. Every time I had a relapse, I simply, lovingly said, "Stop."

I redefined what had happened. The events that had devastated me became opportunities, instead of crises. So, losing my job became a gift that led me to new endeavors. In the three and a half years since I lost my job, I founded a college of teacher education which is about to be authorized to operate; I spent a year as a 5/6 grade classroom teacher in an inner city charter

127

school; and I just got a job as Director of Teacher Education at a local, prestigious university.

Losing my love caused me to readjust my use of time and I wrote, *Heal Yourself Thin,* something I never would have done. It led me to reach out and develop relationships with people who have enriched my life beyond measure, something I hadn't been inclined to do before. And I learned new things about myself in intimate relationships, things which I try to bring to every relationship. I changed my perspective, changed my mind, and changed my life.

With this re-emphasis of my thinking and redirection of my focus, I found happiness. It came from within and has nothing to do with outside circumstances. And anytime I slip into worrying and feeling sorry for myself, I go inward to my faith. I connect with my Divine, and I rediscover my happiness. So I may still be alone, but I'm happy. Even though my monthly paycheck doesn't meet my monthly expenses, I'm happy. I'm happy because I am. I'm happy because I'm not trying to control the world around me. I'm happy because I know that I am being guided and looked after and provided for by God. Nothing could be better than that.

Denise K. Davis' bio follows her story in Chapter 3.

Some Gifts Come Wrapped in Sandpaper
By M.J. Ryan

One of the things that helps when you're going through challenging periods is to recognize, "Alright, I don't know what good thing will come out of this. but I know in the past good has come out of other difficulties."

For instance, I hurt my back when I was 22 years old and I ended up spending a year lying down. My back's hurting me again right now, so I have a vivid recollection of how rotten it is. It was really awful. So I'm not trying to say that when we're going through the hard things, it isn't terrible. It is. But there's always something we are able to learn, experience, develop in ourselves, mentally, emotionally, spiritually, that we wouldn't have; a *Blessing in Disguise*.

One of my clients recently said to me, "I read somewhere that some gifts come wrapped in sandpaper." I love that! I mean that's really what a *Blessing in Disguise* is all about. Sandpaper hurts, it scratches your skin, all you can feel is the discomfort. But at some point, when we're going through the difficulty, we can open the sandpaper and see the gift. That's why we have friends who say cancer or losing their job was the best thing that ever happened to them. At the time, we just think things are horrendous and we'll never survive them. Yet not only do we survive, we cultivate aspects of ourselves that are wonderful.

I looked at numerous studies on 'resilience,' the ability to bounce back from difficulties. Why are some people more resilient than others? There are five qualities that distinguish those who bounce back more easily. One of them is resilient people find meaning in what is happening to them; another way of saying *Blessings in Disguise*. Resilient people know something will come out of what they're going through. They are willing to grow and learn. They have a sense of humor about it. They practice gratitude. They are willing to say, in the moment, "Yes this is terrible, *and* what can I still enjoy and appreciate about my life?"

There are other studies that ask: what can I control? Even though I can't control everything, what *can* I control? What matters more to me more than this thing I'm going through?

The story we tell ourselves about what's happening to us has everything to do with whether or not we're happy or unhappy in the circumstance. That's why somebody like Nelson Mandela can go to jail for 27 years and come out and not be bitter. It's because his story was a story of possibility and hopefulness.

In contrast, Martin Seligman's work on Learned Optimism shows that pessimists tell themselves stories with three dangerous P's. The first is that it's Personal. It's happening only to me. They singled me out. They're out to get me. No one cares about me. The second P is Permanent; it is going to be like this forever. The third is Pervasive. It's not just this part of my life that's miserable, but *all* of my life has been ruined.

To be optimistic we tell ourselves the opposite. One, this is only temporary. It's not permanent. Two, this isn't personal. It's impersonal. For example, losing a job right now has nothing to do with you personally. It has everything to do with the economy. Somebody just told me that she was the top salesperson in her company and she still got laid off because they're laying off everyone. Three, what else can you still enjoy and appreciate in your life, even though this thing really feels awful?

I'm not trying to tell people that it isn't awful. When you're going through a hard time, it's really painful. It's difficult. You thought life was going to go a certain way and then life came and knocked you upside the head and it's turning out to be different. And you feel rotten. So it's important to acknowledge that and to say that feels really terrible, but I need to trust. I need to hope that in the future, it'll be different.

Nelson Mandela never gave up believing that someday he would be free. That's where faith and hope come in. These are spiritual qualities and the difficulty actually helps us grow.

Oftentimes we can't do it on our own. One of the most painful things that ever happened to me was when I was 39 years old, the guy I'd lived with for 14 years dumped me. He came to me one day and said, "I'm not in love with you anymore. Goodbye." We owned a business together, I helped raise his kid from infancy and his decision was totally out of the blue, as far as I was concerned.

I was a total wreck and I told myself, "It's all my fault. I'll never fall in love again. This has ruined my whole life." But one of the things I am good at doing in any difficulty is reaching out for help. So I called everyone I knew and I said, "Help! I'm totally falling apart!" Friends flew in from wherever they were. When I met them at the airport, one friend put his arms around me and said, "Today is someone else's lucky day." I was like, "Huh?" but he was holding the faith; the belief I would fall in love again, that somebody was out there for me.

I was totally convinced that no man would ever love me. This was the same year *Newsweek* came out with an article that said if you're single, forty and female, you're more likely to be struck by lightning than to find a mate. Six months later I met that person and we've been together almost 18 years. That's the *Blessing in Disguise* and why I love to talk about this topic.

You don't know how it's going to turn out. That's the amazing thing. You just don't know. So, in fact, if the guy hadn't dumped me, I wouldn't have my husband or child! I couldn't imagine living without them.

In this instance, I ended up in a wonderful place. I got a new house, new marriage, basically a whole new second life. But sometimes the blessings aren't quite that obvious or concrete. So let's contrast that with what I have learned as a result of my back pain. I've learned patience. I've learned that I have to tend to my body as well as my mind. I have to take care of myself. I used to think that my body was just a taxicab for my brain. I need to be kind and patient with myself. I have to have hope. Those lessons are very valuable, but they're also more amorphous.

Would I rather not have learned them? In a certain way, of course, yes. I've had to go through a lot of physical pain, and still do. But when I focus on the blessing rather than the curse, it makes it a little easier.

However, I don't think you should search for the blessing the day the "bad" thing happens. For instance, last Christmas, I was asked to talk to a Women's CEO networking group about gratitude. I came in and started doing my spiel about gratitude and how fabulous it is, and this woman right across from me burst into tears and left. Afterwards they told me that just before I arrived, she had told the group she was going to have to declare business and personal bankruptcy; not the day for her to listen to a cheery talk on gratitude! It's only later that you can look for the blessings in what's happening.

I always say looking for the blessing is the 'graduate school of gratitude' because it can only happen when you're ready. It can't be forced. You have to be in that place in which you can be willing to say, "If anything could be good about this, if anything could be right about this, if anything could be useful to me about this, what is it?"

One of the most interesting things I've found was research that shows we can simultaneously mourn and move on. We don't have to go through our entire grieving process before we get up and say, "Okay, now what? How can I put my life back together?" I remember both falling in love and still being in grief simultaneously. Just because I met someone six months later did not mean I was done mourning the end of my old relationship.

The man I'm now married to was okay with that. He understood that my crying because of the end of my former relationship didn't mean I didn't love him. I had a lot of emotional work to do that couldn't be bypassed.

So how do you do that? How to you simultaneously mourn and move on? It comes back to finding meaning in what's happening, believing in a positive outcome, being willing to grow and learn, having humor and practicing gratitude. We've discovered these qualities can be learned and used by anyone. What am I thankful for today? What good can come out of this? How can I actually use this in a positive way?

For people who find themselves mourning without moving on, remember everyone goes through these things in their own way and in their own time. Whenever you're encountering something that's a challenge, you need support. If you find yourself stuck in the grieving process, perhaps you need a good therapist or something else. It's not 'do you need support' but 'what kind of support do you need?'

Social psychologists have actually defined the types of support humans require. There's 'circumstantial support' like money or a place to live or food. There's 'emotional support,' someone who listens and helps you deal with your feelings, which could be therapy or a compassionate friend. Then there's 'mental support' which might be help brainstorming ideas. 'Alright, this isn't working. What else can you do?' You may need help thinking clearer than you're able to think at the moment. Ask yourself, 'what kind of support do I need?' and then 'where can I get it?'

Some people have a happy temperament and that's great. They don't have to work as hard at being happy. But for the rest of us, the key is to understand it is really, truly about the stories that we tell ourselves and how we interpret reality. It's how we cultivate our own sense of happiness.

Happiness, since Aristotle, has been defined as coming from one of two paths. The 'path of fulfillment' which is about using your gifts and talents to the maximum, and the 'path of contentment' which is about simple pleasures, appreciation and enjoyment, like hot baths and chocolate ice cream kind of happiness. Knowing these two pathways, we can ask ourselves how well we do in each. Do you have enough pleasures in your life? Do you need more fulfillment? Do you need a greater sense of meaning and purpose? The internal places are where happiness is found and when we find our minds wandering off into worry... what if...I don't have enough...*stop*! In this moment, how are you? Right *now*, everything's okay.

Inspirational author and coach M.J. Ryan is one of the creators of the New York Times bestselling Random Acts of Kindness series and the author of AdaptAbility: How to Survive Change You Didn't Ask For, This Year I Will...., The Happiness Makeover, Attitudes of Gratitude, The Power of Patience, Trusting Yourself, The Giving Heart, *and* 365 Health and Happiness Boosters, *among other titles. Ryan is the life coach columnist for* Health *and a contributing editor to* Good Housekeeping. *She has appeared on "The Today Show," CNN, and hundreds of radio programs. Renown as a change expert, she works with Professional Thinking Partners and specializes in coaching individuals and teams around the world.*

STEPPING STONES

The truth is that events are neither 'bad' nor 'good'. They simply are. We are not in a position to accurately evaluate what's going on, when it's going on.

When adversity strikes, you have several options:

1. You can fret, stress out and get sucked into the drama. Be a victim! Call all your friends! Alert the media! (If this is your typical response, how's that working out for you?)

2. You can do what you can to detach from assessing what's going on. Who are you to say that this particular event is 'good' or 'bad'? You don't know. You might not know for many years.

3. If you can't cease judgment, postpone it. (Well this seems 'bad' but I'm going to wait and see how this turns out, eventually). Besides, this may well be a short-term circumstance.

4. You can strive for the bigger picture. Yes, you're fired/ sick/in debt/grieving. Yes, it hurts. But this doesn't define you in your entirety, for all time. You are more than the pain you are experiencing.

5. You can look for opportunities to be grateful, regardless of what's going on. While any challenge is going on, the rest of your life continues. You are still loved, you still love others. Other areas of your life are flourishing. To the extent that you can shift your attention to them, you will have an easier time navigating difficult waters.

6. You can actively look for potential blessings in the experience. New directions? New relationships? New insights? Healthier ways of being?

7. You can put your trust in larger forces. It may seem trite to say 'I'm handing this over to the universe/to God/to fate' but sometimes, that's the only option. When you truly surrender the illusion of control over the situation, you will feel relief from the pain.

8. You can believe that everything is unfolding, exactly as it should, for your highest and best good. You can believe that, whatever you're going through, blessings are emerging.

Activity: Think of a 'Blessing in Disguise' in your own life – some challenge or apparent setback that ended up turning out for the best. What happened?

_____

_____

_____

_____

How did you handle it, at the time it was going on?

_____

_____

_____

_____

What blessings emerged, eventually?

_____

_____

_____

_____

If you were to go back through the initial incident (now that you know how things would turn out eventually), how would you handle it?

_____

_____

_____

_____

What lessons can you take from this, going forward? How can you better approach life's challenges, as they arise?

_____

_____

_____

_____

Activity: Quick! Think of some issue in your life at the moment. (Whatever you think of first is perfect). Now, take a moment and write four things in your life about which you are grateful:

_____

_____

_____

_____

Thinking of the same issue, write four possible blessings you can imagine coming out of the experience:

_____

_____

_____

_____

Activity: We always have some issue we can point to—just as we always have reasons to be grateful. Take a moment to think about one or more issues in your life – take note of the icky, negative sensations in your body. Now, take a moment to think about one or more blessings in your life. Note how you feel now. Isn't that better? Your body can serve as a guidance system: Whenever you find yourself feeling 'icky', shift to thinking about the things in your life that are going well.

Activity: Any incident provides opportunities for blessings – and any incident can spark a course correction towards happiness. Take a moment to write down examples of both you have experienced in your life.

_____

_____

_____

_____

CHAPTER 7

Have I Lived Before?

While many people do not believe in reincarnation, anyone who is seeking a better understanding of their emotions and life's mysteries should take the time to explore the theory and consider the possibilities it presents.

In order to do that you will need to abandon any preconceived notions about reincarnation and read this chapter with an open mind. In other words, pretend that you do believe you may have lived before and read the explanations and stories in this chapter. At the end of it, if you still cannot accept it, you are free to return to your old way of thinking. It is possible that you are a person who is living his or her very first lifetime. After all, everyone has to start somewhere.

For many years now, doctors have used regression therapy to treat patients with crippling fears that cannot otherwise be explained. The many books and articles on the subject say that the subconscious mind is like a tape recorder set to automatically record everything that happens during a person's lifetime. It is part of your soul or your inner spirit and stays with you throughout each of your incarnations. So, if a child is bitten by a dog, for example, that incident could foster an aversion and fear of dogs that may be difficult to overcome. That's because any time a dog approaches, the subconscious mind remembers the pain and fear of the first attack and telegraphs that emotion to the conscious mind. If the trauma is deep enough, this fear can be carried forward into the person's next lifetime as well. Have you known a child who screams hysterically whenever a dog gets near even if he or she has never been bitten or frightened by one?

Next consider the fact that you have probably met a new person and taken an instant dislike to him or her. On the other hand, another new person sparks an immediate warmth in you. Why does that happen? The theory of reincarnation suggests that is because you are encountering people in your current lifetime that you knew in a past life. Once again your subconscious mind or your inner spirit has retained a memory of the past life relationship and sent a signal to the conscious mind that either accepts or rejects people you have known before.

One of the basic beliefs in the study of reincarnation is that the same souls come together again and again to learn from each other and work out problems they shared in a prior lifetime. It's like a couple that marries and divorces and then marries each other again, striving to make their relationship work despite prior adversities.

It is said that we are all on this earth to love and to learn. So, if we fail to learn specific lessons in one lifetime, we come back and try again. There are religions that reject this theory because they claim we only have one chance to attain our heavenly rewards. Failure to live a good life results in being damned for eternity. People who believe in reincarnation cling to the theory that God loves us so much that we can come back to earth over and over again to love and learn the lessons that will eventually bring our souls to perfection.

Another belief is that someone who has loved us in a prior lifetime will come into our current lifetime to help us learn a specific lesson. It is also thought that a person who has done us harm in another lifetime may assume a prominent role in a new incarnation to make up for the pain caused in a past life. One of the stories in this chapter tells of just such a happening.

People who are experiencing loss and many problems in their current lifetime may decide that being on earth is too difficult. They will be glad to shed their bodies and never return to earth again. Reincarnation is not believed to be mandatory. Each soul has a choice to return again and learn more lessons or remain in the spirit world at whatever level their last life has attained for them. Guardian angels are considered master spirits with an abundance of love and wisdom who have chosen to help us in our current lifetime.

One of the most comforting aspects of reincarnation is the belief that tragedies are not punishments but simply a way in which our souls learn our lessons. How else can you explain the atrocities of life and still believe in a loving God?

If you are unsure about reincarnation there are many books you can read that may help dispel your doubts and delve deeper into the theories and beliefs about whether or not you have lived before.

Trapped In a Castle
By Maggie TerryViale

My friend placed a few acupuncture needles in me. My heart, on an emotional level, was hurting and there were symptoms of anger, too. I knew the anger was about my latest relationship that wasn't going well. For some odd reason, the feeling of being trapped would come over me whenever I stayed at his house.

All at once, I was back in a prior lifetime when we were together. He seemed to be a ruler of some sort and I was his daughter. This time what I saw was myself with very long hair, down to my waist. It hung free over my shoulders, but I was not free. I rode a white horse, side-saddle, but I was being led by someone appointed to watch me. There were other eyes watching my every move, too. It was sunny, a beautiful day, and I gazed out at the distant forest where I longed to ride. I wanted to ride free, but instead I was being led around a courtyard. Going into the open forest was forbidden by my father.

Evidently I had tried to run away before because I felt envy for the poor in town, for they were, it seemed to me, free and happy to do as they pleased. What a wasted life, I thought. I had everything, all of the servants, all of the wealth that one could ask for, but I was a kept young woman of 16 and all of my decisions were not mine. They were made by my father, who was the same person I was having difficulties with in my current life.

What could I do to change things, I wondered, as the acupuncture needles were doing their healing work on me? How could I have been happy then and again in my present life with this person? I decided to change how I was feeling about the past life I was experiencing. I chose to be happy. I decided to feel the warmth of the sunshine on me as I was led around in circles on the back of this beautiful horse. I decided to be grateful for a father who was concerned about me. But most of all I decided to reconnect with God, and let Divine love flow through me. I felt sighs and shudders of relief flow through my body. My heart felt lighter.

I decided to forgive my father in that lifetime, and most of all I decided to forgive myself, as well.

I don't know on what level my relationship with this person from my past will continue in the present, but I do know I now feel freer, happier, and appreciative of this past life experience. I've always known that money, riches, and even a castle don't make a person happy. And maybe there has been a part of me that was blocking material possessions, too.

Now I know I am free. Free to enjoy life more, all because of a few needles, and a dear healer friend who assisted me in opening my heart and spirit to uncovering deeper issues that stemmed from a past life. I thank her for the gift she has given me.

Maggie TerryViale is a co-author of this book.

Learning from the Past
By Carol Costa

My study of reincarnation and the books that I had read on the subject prompted me to seek out a reputable person and see if I could be regressed to a prior lifetime. Unlike many people who go into a regression session looking for answers and help for difficulties and unexplained fears, I was simply doing it to confirm my growing belief in the theory. I had a good life and felt that I was pretty well adjusted and happy in it.

Being regressed meant being put into a relaxed hypnotic state where I could access the information stored in my subconscious. The regression therapist first asked me a series of questions about my life, my health, and my emotional state. That reassured me that she was concerned about my welfare and I was anxious to begin.

"One thing I must stress," the therapist told me before we began. "You must promise me that you will tell me the very first thought that comes into your mind. Just blurt it out."

I soon came to understand why she had been so adamant about that. The thoughts that surface from the subconscious mind must pass through the conscious mind and the conscious mind tends to question and analyze everything it receives. As you will soon learn, it was a struggle for me to turn off the warnings and opinions of my conscious mind and follow the therapist's instructions.

Just before she began the process of hypnotizing me, the therapist told me that I would probably go back to the lifetime that I needed to know about right now and for me that turned out to be very true.

In the hypnotic state that I attained the first thing I saw were white lights flashing and coming towards me.

"Spirits often appear to us as lights. Concentrate on the brightest light and tell me what comes into your mind," the therapist told me.

"Rocco Blasi," I said immediately.

"Who is Rocco Blasi?"

"My uncle, my mother's brother who died before I was born."

"Is he giving you a message?"

"He says that he is the one who sent me into this lifetime to be with my mother. His death devastated her and I was sent to heal the pain. I was chosen because I was similar to him in intellect and personality."

"Your uncle is your spirit guide, a master spirit."

Although I had never thought about who my spirit guide could be or even considered Uncle Rocco as a possibility, I knew a great deal about him. My mother and others in my family talked about him all the time. He was a brilliant student, a writer, and an incorrigible practical joker. Having lost their mother at an early age, Uncle Rocco and my mom were very close. His death at the age of 27 had been a terrible blow to her. After a routine appendectomy, peritonitis had set in and since this was in the days before penicillin, Rocco died. My mother told me that as he was dying his many friends and relatives came to say good-bye. He told them all not to cry for him as it was time for him to leave and he was happy about it.

Before the therapist moved me backwards away from Uncle Rocco, he told me that whenever I needed him, all I had to do was think about him and he would be there to guide me.

Now I traveled back through my current life and saw the joy my birth had brought to my parents. The therapist now instructed me to move farther back in time.

"Where are you?" the therapist asked.

"I'm in Maine."

"What year is it?"

"1907."

"What are you doing?"

"I'm outside with other children, dancing around, playing some sort of game."

"What is your name?"

"Susan."

"What is your last name?"

The name Brown leapt into my mind and that's when my subconscious mind started to protest. Can't you think of something better than that? Ignoring the taunt, I repeated my name to the therapist. "Brown. My name is Susan Brown."

We went on to explore where I was in Maine, a town called Bountiful, a place where my family had come to escape the religious persecution in Europe. My father was a minister in this small colony of people settled on the coast of Maine. I recalled looking out the upstairs window of our house at the ocean crashing against the rocks on the shoreline. My conscious mind told me that this scene was depicted in paintings that I had always been drawn to. Now I understood why those paintings held so much appeal for me.

The therapist moved me forward in this lifetime to my teenage years and that's when the trouble began. I felt my abdomen swelling and a strong pressure much like labor pains.

"Oh my God," I blurted out. "I think Susan is pregnant. She's in labor."

As I concentrated on that, I saw myself lying on a table in a room. I was indeed in labor and a woman was standing over me watching me struggle.

"Where are your parents?" the therapist asked.

"They are ashamed of me. I have sinned and they have washed their hands of me."

"Who is the father of your baby?"

The first name that came into my mind was, Frank, my husband in this lifetime and as I considered this I saw him clearly in the group of children I had danced with in my first memory of this past life. I spoke his name aloud and told the therapist that I was married to him now.

"Why isn't he with Susan?"

"He's dead, killed in the War."

At this point, let me tell you that American History has never been my strong suit. I really had no idea if there was a war going on in 1917 or not. As I learned later, it was World War I that was being fought at that time.

My labor pains were getting stronger and I cried out. The therapist instructed me to rise above it, move forward and relive the experience from a distance.

"What is happening now?" she prompted.

"I died. My baby and I both died." I was free of the physical pain but now the emotion of dying and taking my unborn child with me overwhelmed me.

"Where are you?" the therapist asked sharply.

"I'm with my baby. I know her. It's Maria. She's telling me not to be upset that we will have another chance and in our next lifetime we will be happy together."

"Who is Maria?"

"Maria is my youngest daughter, my surprise child," I replied suddenly understanding so much about my current life because of this journey back to my past life.

After having three children in five years, my husband and I decided not to have any more. Then, when our youngest child was eight years old, I discovered I was pregnant. At that time this came as more of a shock than a surprise, but Maria Lynn turned out to be a lovely delightful child who brought much happiness to everyone in our family. Because the other children were so much older, they were out on their own by the time Maria was a teenager and she and I were very close and shared many happy times together.

As for Frank, he took care of me and our kids so well, working two jobs whenever it was necessary, always helping with housework and the kids. He had left me alone and pregnant in our last lifetime together, but now I knew he was making up for it in this lifetime. When I thought back on how we had gotten together, I knew that it was meant to be, but that's another story.

My regression session ended with more questions and answers and information that could be checked out and verified. I saw my tombstone in a small cemetery. It simply said Susan Brown, 1901-1917.

My last life had been a short sad one, but it had evolved into my current life. Two other souls had moved forward with me giving me all the love and support I had missed out on as Susan Brown.

As I had been told before the regression began, most people went back to memories of the life that they needed to revisit in order to help them now. That was very true for me.

I have been regressed several times since that first session and have learned much more about myself and why I feel and act as I do today. I have never gone back to my life as Susan Brown again, but I think that's because I have learned all I needed to know from that incarnation.

Carol Costa is a co-author of this book.

"My, Aren't You Brave...."
By Maggie TerryViale

It was during the Los Angeles South Central riots. The stillness of the small Seal Beach community was uncannily eerie. Gray flakes of ash and smoke mingled with distant gunfire. Everyone was home, locked inside, and glued to the events on TV. But I had to go to the beach. I was returning home and running across the greenbelt on Electric Ave.

There were no cars on the street at 7 pm until a convertible full of young men drove slowly by. My eyes locked with a stranger sitting in the back seat and he spoke to me.

"My, aren't you brave...."

His words instantly transported me into another world and another time and place.

I'm running across a field, both watching and feeling it at the same time. I see her clearly, a slight woman with long, deep, hair pulled back into a loose bun. She wears a simple long skirt and holds the hand of her eight-year-old boy. Together they run for their lives. It's another country, another era. There is no shelter, no place to hide, only dying, marshy fields shattered by war. I hear it coming from behind us; the unmistakable guttural sound of a military helicopter. It only takes a moment. We lay bloodied in our homeland of Vietnam.

I rise out of my body and pass through the helicopter's metal walls. I hear the gunner laughing. We had been mere hunting sport for him. But a young stranger sits in the back, hysterical.

"You killed them; an innocent mother and child. You killed them."

The gunner laughs louder as he scans the fields for another target. The young stranger can't get the bloodied, mangled, image of our slain bodies out of his mind. He swore no more killings. I knew my death had changed him forever. My death moved him toward peace. I felt gratitude that I was part of his transformation.

"My, aren't you brave to be out here all alone on a night like this." It was said with sincerity, and as the car passed, I remembered who the stranger was.

I looked after the car and smiled. Dear Stranger, how nice to meet again. I'm so glad your point of view has changed, you are now a peaceful man and I'm honored to be part of your journey. I walked slowly towards my beach apartment, smiling, happy just to be alive.

And the deep guttural sound of military helicopters never bothered me again.

Maggie TerryViale is a co-author of this book.

Group Sessions
By Carol Costa

One of the first books I read on reincarnation was *Many Lives, Many Masters*, by Brian L. Weiss M.D. Dr. Weiss is a clincal psycologist who had no interest in past life regressions until the day a patient he was treating regressed to another lifetime during his session with her. The patient told Dr. Weiss about long ago events in the doctor's private life that she had no possible way of knowing.

From this patient, Dr Weiss learned about spirit guides and their place in each of our lives and it prompted the doctor to begin an indepth study of reincarnation and regression therapy. What I liked most about *Many Lives, Many Masters* is that the book did not try to convince the reader that he or she had lived before. It simply reported the doctor's experience and the information he uncovered through his research and regression sessions with patients.

The first time I was regressed I learned a lot about myself and how some of the feelings and behavior patterns I have in this life are based on my experiences in my past life. I also learned that people in my past life are with me again this time around.

Anxious to know more about my past lives, I enrolled in a class being offered at the community college taught by a therapist who specialized in past life regression.

I had my doubts as to what could come out of a group regression session, but I have to say that I learned a lot from the memories that surfaced in me and from the ones that other people in the class shared during the sessions.

I learned that my dislike and refusal to enter a cave in this lifetime resulted from a past life where I lived in a cave and ran out of it every chance I got into the forest. In another lifetime, I saw myself as a young girl living in a quaint thatched cottage with my family.

I was about to leave the family and marry an older man who would take me to London.

As I was packing, I went to my dresser and removed a collection of manuscripts that

the man had promised to help me publish. So, my current lifetime is not the first one in which I was a writer.

Is it possible that these memories stem from another source other than a past life? I suppose it is, but somehow I believe that they are true events that I actually experienced and am able to recall under hypnosis or during deep meditation.

While my deaths in some of these lifetimes were unexpected, early, and tragic, they didn't have a negative effect on the overall regression experiences and what I learned from them.

In one session, we were told to picture ourselves on a lovely beach near the sea. As I stood watching the waves come onto the shore, I saw images of my children who came to me and expressed their love and joy at being with me again in my current lifetime.

Who can argue over the benefits of experiencing something so lovely and profound.

Am I recommending that you find a therapist and get regressed? Certainly not. What works for one person, may not work for another. Regression and the study of reincarnation were simply my personal search for knowledge and understanding. I am recommending that you open yourself up to new experiences and embrace the good people and things you have in this lifetime.

Carol Costa is a co-author of this book.

It Happened
By Maggie TerryViale

It was the late 70's, I had never heard of past lives, nor reincarnation before but a flyer arrived in my mailbox. A woman was writing a book and wanted to do a study on past lives. Would I want to participate? The cost was prohibited on my budget, but it seemed interesting. I read the flyer and in it, she outlined the steps she used to regress people. I thought, well, if this is true, I should be able to regress myself and save some money.

I sat down cross legged in my home and reread the details. At the time I was living in a home that overlooked the Carquinez Straits, a part of the San Francisco Bay. It was always damp, almost too damp for me, and the hills, were green with stoic, twisted oak trees. I began to count myself down, just as instructed. I felt a twirling energy out the top of my crown. I continued.

Suddenly I felt it. The arid heat, and the scratchy material that felt like burlap on my back. My hair was disheveled and I could feel sand mingled with the tangled mane. I looked down; my feet were bare and enormous. My legs were chained; I was crouched on my haunches, a giant of a deformed being captured in the desert, surrounded by miles of sand. In the near distance, a camp of laughing men. Were they laughing at me? I felt miserable.

A man from the camp came up to me with a plate of food. He gave it to me. "Here. Eat. Poisonous food." was all he said.

I knew he was giving me a choice. I could end my misery. I did not see what happened next because I came back into my current life, and felt the moisture against my face. I made drawings of this lifetime and have always remembered it. Was it proof that I have lived before? It was to me.

Years later, I was teaching at a children's school in Sedona, Arizona. It was a gorgeous day and a couple of teachers and I sat watching the children play. One 5 year old girl came up behind me. She held my long blonde hair out wide around my head, and said, "I want you to roar. You're a lion." We laughed, I roared. Had she known somehow that I was a double Leo?

Next she led me by the hand to stand under the wooden jungle gym. There in the sand, she pointed and said, "Sit." I played along and squatted down on my haunches. Next she motioned like she was giving me something, I accepted.

"Here. Eat. Poisonous food," she told me.

Was she, could it be, that we had met again? Was she the man in the camp? I can't say for sure, all I can say is it happened.

Maggie TerryViale is a co-author of this book.

STEPPING STONES

Meditation is a good way to reach into your subconscious mind and identify and rectify any fears or phobia's that are causing problems in your life. Start by writing down your fears and concerns which will bring them out in the open and allow you to face them head on.

_____

_____

_____

_____

The method of meditation you choose is up to you. There are countless books on the market to help and instruct you. Start with what you feel is the simplest problem you need to solve and work your way up to the bigger things.

If you are unable to meditate on your own, find a person to help you get started. Like anything else, achieving a level of meditation deep enough to help you may take time and practice.

Make a list of things that you find soothing and comforting and see how you can use them to meditate. Refer to the chapter, Are We There Yet? for information and suggestions on meditating.

_____

_____

_____

_____

If you have a person in your life who is causing you problems, try through meditation to put yourself into that's person's shoes to better understand why they are acting in a way that distresses you.

Remember that we are all part of the Universe and trust in God, and the love and mercy of your family and friends to help you overcome your fears and problems.

If you are so inclined, find a reputable therapist and let him or her regress you.

CHAPTER 8

Are We There Yet?

Isn't that the classic question heard from a child in the back seat of a car? And adults often have the same question regarding, well, what adults consider to be more important things. For example, someone who has worked as a struggling artist, hairdresser, actress, accountant, or any other career may ask, why don't I have all of the money, processions, clientele, and fame that I deserve? What in the world is the holdup? By my age, I should have been there my now.

The same is true of our spiritual path. You may have read the books, gone to the religious affiliations of your choice, studied, practiced, prayed, fasted, meditated even, and be asking where is my halo? I should be up there with Buddha by now. And, please, don't tell me all I need is more patience.

But what if it's like being on a road trip; it's not the destination that counts, it's the journey. Can you find happiness right here, right now, where you are? When you think about it, what else is there? You can't be happy in the future, nor in the past. This moment it is your choice to be, or not to be, happy, satisfied, at least ok with, where you are on your path.

Once you have accepted that life is a journey, pressure melts away like a block of ice in the desert sun. Gone is the hard block of resistance, and left in its place is cool, refreshing water to nourish our souls.

Over time we know ourselves better. Over time we learn what makes us feel good, what warms our hearts. We are all unique. You may learned over time that walking through a nursery and gazing at plants, or buying fresh flowers for your table, or taking a quiet break to center and listen to Guidance transforms you. Certain colors, like yellow, may make your spirit soar and the silence of nature can soothe your soul.

What is your personal truth? What makes your heart sing? In this chapter we will explore ways to make our spiritual journey more enjoyable.

Scripting the Perfect Life
By D. H. Palmer

Do you want to have a life that is like a well scripted movie with gorgeous scenery, colorful costumes, and brilliant dialogue, and filled with all things positive that you can imagine for yourself and your loved ones? I know I do. I have wanted this since I was a little girl. Deep in my soul I knew it was possible, but I did not know how to achieve it. Although basic religious teachings taught suffering, hardship, and worse, I knew in my heart that somewhere out there I would find roadmaps to lead me to my promised land, the beautiful movie script that I called, My Perfect Life.

Controlling your thoughts is the way you script for control of your life. And the positive is where you need to place your power. Clara Palmer expressed the path to the positive in the following quote, "Every word of truth you think or speak is a power for good. It works immediately to create new conditions of harmony, righteousness, health, and peace."

Coming to the realization that I was the one who controlled my life was a moment of incredible freedom and awesome responsibility. I knew the moment I understood how the system worked, I could no longer blame anyone or anything for the mishaps or good fortune I experienced.

When you are honest with yourself, you will admit you have been guilty of blaming outside influences for the mishaps in your life. In other words, you have been reluctant to take ownership of your life. I will confide that I used to, and you can console yourself in the knowledge that most people do use a myriad of excuses for why their life is messed up. Realize that you and only you are in control of your life.

At times it is maddening, because a thought refuses to go in the assigned file drawer in my head. I have had to actually come up with little mind games to hush up the repetitive ranting that sometimes threaten my sanity and my sleep pattern. Meditating is a wonderful way to get back on track, but requires a quiet space, and lets face it, sometimes life is pretty darn busy. So, I developed a few tricks to keep myself on track.

One trick is what I call my alphabet game. In my head, while I am in the middle of doing any number of chores or activities, I can start with the letter *A* and think of positive words that start with *A*. I usually start with the word Angel because I personally like the idea that I have a whole legion of these blessed beings to guide me and help me. If I am not being extremely creative I may resort to words like apple, artichoke, animal, etc. Remember you can only select positive or neutral words. Once you catch yourself struggling for more positive words for that letter, then move on to the next. You have a full 26 letters to use and can do the whole exercise again if your mind is still trying to trouble you with that less than positive thought. I suspect that it is sort of like the old trick our parents and teachers taught us about the concept of counting to ten before answering. You may have your own method for self control and can certainly make up any type of system that will help you gain control over your emotions and keep you in the positive mode as much as is possible. You in essence are taking control of your creative mind.

When I write TV scripts I am also playing a small God part because from beginning to end I control such things as the timing, dialogue, commercial spots, and camera angles. Nothing is left to chance or the whim of the stars. Oh yes, there could be an unexpected delay, i.e., breaking news of some sort, but one way or the other the show will happen as it is scripted.

Therefore, see yourself as not only a script writer but also as the Producer of Your Perfect Life; think about all the aspects that go into putting on your entire production. It's Your Life. When planning a play or TV script one must think about all of the following:
   a. Set location
   b. Costume or dress
   c. Dialogue
   d. Music

    e. Lighting

    f. Timing

    g. Preparation and rehearsal time

Realize that all of these things are important to create the foundation on which one builds the production of a perfectly completed show. Would you not like to have your life be a well scripted and beautifully done positive experience? I am sure your answer would be a resounding yes. I am sure that you want to be joyous, prosperous and healthy. Look at the list above and fill in or change the words to fit your version of what you want in your life.

At a certain point in my life after having read many quotes from the Bible, not to mention volumes and volumes of spiritual and self-help books, I decided I wanted to be in control of my life, totally in control. I guess you could say I wanted to be the author of my own script and be the writer, director, and producer of *My Perfect Life*. If I can do this, you can do this.

As I stated earlier, I wish to help you give this gift of a happy life to the most deserving person you know, you! I will spell out in simple terms how to begin on your journey. So here it goes.

Simply stated, the happy life you seek is your gift to yourself. Your journey can be achieved with a KISS. Now I have my own interpretation of that familiar acronym, KISS. The meaning for me is: Keep it Spiritually Simple.

1. Believe you are in control of your life. Believe in yourself.

2. Do not try to blame your parents, second grade teacher, college professor or spouse for any of your problems. Take ownership.

3. Own up to the fact that you are the one who has created all of what has happened to you whether it is good or bad. Acknowledge that it is all in the past and let it go. Live in the Present.

4. Decide you are starting fresh as of this moment. Take action now and create perfection.

5. Acknowledge the God force within you and use this incredible creative power to   create what you want in your life. Create your joy.
6. Accept the fact that your mind controls what you create. Creative positive in your life.
7. Think unselfish and positive thoughts. Use discipline to control your thoughts.
8. Know that in doing so you get happy positive events. Use the power of attraction and expect great results.
9. Know if you think lack, sickness, turmoil, etc. you will get these things. Create abundance, joy and peace.
10. Pay close attention to how you feel. Use your inner wisdom.

So remember to use KISS all the time, Keep it Spiritually Simple. Whatever your spirituality is founded upon whether it be Christianity, Judaism, Buddhism, Hinduism, etc. you can take a short but simple precept that you feel sums up the core of your belief and use that as your mantra of simplicity. My mantra that I bring to mind whenever needed is: "I am a spiritual being, living in a spiritual universe and governed by spiritual law." Do what works for you.

D.H. Palmer's bio follows her first story in Chapter 2.

Becoming a Joy Spreader
By Barbara Schiffman, C.Ht.

"Your real job in this life is to be a Joy Spreader…"

These words suddenly popped into my mind as I stepped into the parking garage elevator at my hypnotherapy office. As the doors slid together and the elevator started to descend the 5 floors to street level, I wondered where it came from. It didn't feel like a thought from my subconscious or even a message from my Inner Guides. Was I having a conversation with God?

Over the past four decades, I've had dozens of jobs and several concurrent careers. I've been an assistant to Hollywood agents and producers, a Creative Executive to famous Hollywood hyphenates, a script consultant to top cable and film companies, a career breakthrough coach, a life balance coach, a certified hypnotherapist and most recently an Akashic Records consultant. But this was the first time I'd seemingly been given a job by my Higher Self, even though the focus of my work as a Life & Soul coach is to support people in boosting and strengthening their own positive energy from the inside out.

My next unbidden thought was that even though I do a lot of things and have been trained in a wide range of healing and counseling techniques, my cosmic mission is merely to spread joy wherever I go, to everyone I encounter. No matter what else I say or do, if I consciously spread joy, I'm fulfilling my purpose for being.

As a young woman who seemed rather anxious joined me on the elevator, I tested out my new assignment by smiling at her and thinking about spreading joy. I consciously shifted myself into a state of quiet joyfulness and silently projected it in her direction, radiating it outward like an invisible rainbow. She suddenly glanced over at me and smiled back. I felt great sharing what the French call "joie de vivre" (the joy of life) starting with one smile in that small elevator.

I quickly realized that no matter what I do for a living, my soul assignment is not an action; it's a state of being that we're all born with but too quickly forget. So I accepted the cosmic job of being a Joy Spreader from that moment on. It's been empowering and transforming for me and seemingly for those who receive the joy I spread with a smile, a kind word or deed, or just a projected energy flow. It feels at times like I'm wearing a pair of rose colored glasses that no one butme can see or I'm spraying Joy perfume into the air like one of those perfume girls in cosmetics departments.

Being a Joy Spreader has definitely shifted how I respond to strangers. When I remember who I really am, Joy Spreader #101, the world looks and feels better. But all that's really changed is my attitude and perspective. By spreading joy, I know I'm shifting the energy of the whole planet through uplifting one person at a time. Every bit of Joy counts!

You can become a Joy Spreader too just by accepting this cosmic assignment. There's plenty of Joy to be spread around, and a growing need for it. So it's a job that won't get downsized anytime soon.

See what happens when you begin consciously tapping your inner wellspring of joy. It may feel like you've taken a Happiness pill. All you need to do is feel it and then share it through a smile or an encouraging word. Notice if the atmosphere shifts as it did for me that first time in the elevator. Don't be surprised if people smile back or just perk up by being near you. If so, you're doing your new job well.

Being a Joy Spreader is also fun when you go to a party or a new place where people are anxious or in a rush. Just by consciously shifting into a joyful state you uplift the energy for everyone in the room. Being joyful doesn't require being noisy or showy. It is often as simple and unobtrusive as just feeling good about being alive and being you.

I hope you enjoy this new full-time life-long job as much as I do. If we all spread joy wherever we go, imagine how joyful the whole world will be!

Barbara Schiffman, C.Ht., is a Certified Hypnotherapist, Life & Soul Coach, Akashic Records Consultant/Teacher and Hollywood script consultant/creative producer. She is also a published author and public speaker specializing in life balance and growing your soul. Visit her website www.HypnoSynergy. com for info on her guided meditation CD kits and also to access her internet radio show, Living in Balance. *She can be reached for information on private or group sessions, teleclasses and workshops at 818-415-3479.*

Hopi Elders' Prophecy
Oraibi, Arizona, June 8, 2000

You have been telling people that this is the Eleventh Hour, now you must go back and tell the people that this is the Hour. And there are things to be considered

Where are you living?
What are you doing?
What are your relationships?
Are you in right relation?
Where is your water?
Know your garden.
It is time to speak your truth.

Create your community.
Be good to each other.
And do not look outside yourself for your leader.

Then he clasped his hands together, smiled, and said, "This could be a good time! There is a river flowing now very fast. It is so great and swift that there are those who will be afraid.

They will try to hold on to the shore. They will feel they are being torn apart and will suffer greatly. Know the river has its destination. The elders say we must let go of the shore, push off into the middle of the river, keep our eyes open, and our heads above the water.

And I say, see who is in there with you and celebrate. At this time in history, we are to take nothing personally, least of all ourselves. For the moment that we do, our spiritual growth and journey come to a halt.

The time of the lone wolf is over. Gather yourselves!
Banish the word 'struggle' from your attitude and your
vocabulary. All that we do now must be done in a sacred
manner and in celebration.
We are the ones we've been waiting for.

*From this prophecy we learn to be good to one another and to
look at ourselves as leaders.*

Connecting with the Spirit
By John Sackett

We are always connected to God, the universe, and all of life. It's our natural state. Running around here and there, worrying about what we think is important causes us to feel out of touch or disconnected from what is real.

Energy interaction comes from the fact that we pass through many energy fields through out the course of a day. Our own energy fields act like magnets for the energy of others. Some of the outside energies we attract can cause an emotional imbalance in our lives. Meditation cleanses you of negative energy and allows you to recover and maintain emotional balance and stability.

Meditation is a way to reconnect with whatever you believe is a greater power. You can call it God, the Great Spirit, your higher self, the sun, the moon, life itself or anything else that makes sense to you. Your definitions of Spirit may change from time to time. Allow it. In the end, what you call it doesn't matter at all. What matters is that you feel it and it exists for you at any given moment.

The following meditation exercise is offered as a pathway in your meditation journey. If you are not sure what you need at the moment, close your eyes and ask your higher self, "What do I need at this time?" Trust what you receive from the Waterfall of Light.

See yourself standing on a flat rock at the bottom of a very tall golden waterfall.

Step into the falls and feel the liquid light flowing down through you and around you. Feel the power of it.

Say the words: "I release, I release, I release!"

As more of your negative energy is released, you become lighter and you rise up through the waterfall. Breathe in the light. Stay as long as you like. When you are ready to end your meditation, come back down, gently landing on the flat rock.

John Sackett is a Conscious Channel working with the Angels, Archangels, Ascended Masters and other evolved beings of light. At the request of the Masters he started a weekly Channeled Meditation Group in New York in 1994. He continued the weekly "meditations" for 12 years until he moved to Cave Creek, Arizona. He now makes these teachings available in the Phoenix area and is also available for readings. Contact him by email: matrixxboy3@gmail.com

Pass It On
By Kitty Chappell

The air in the choir room was heavy with silence. The group collectively held its breath. Only the sound of the air conditioner broke the stillness with its gentle hum, pouring out cool, refreshing air that was suddenly needed.

Lisa stood motionless. Manicured from her golden hair to her stylish shoes, she was an attractive woman who was not growing old without a fight. She waged a strong battle against this inevitability and appeared to be holding her own. Frozen into silence by embarrassment, she stood stoically—a gentle elegant statue. With wounded doe eyes, she stared helplessly in shock at Harry, the perpetrator of her pain.

Ruddy-faced and unaware of his abrasive effect on others, Harry waged his own battles. He fought a terminal case of hoof and mouth disease. Actually he rarely fought. Maybe it was because when he did put up a feeble fight, he usually lost. In typical fashion, Harry had interrupted a private conversation between Lisa and another female choir member as they planned a luncheon date to celebrate Lisa's upcoming birthday.

"You are going to be HOW old?" he bellowed, loud enough to be heard in the parking lot. Harry's question typically arose more from a desire to obtain fodder for his insensitive humor than from any real interest in her age. Lisa responded honestly. Following her response, Harry proclaimed loudly, "Well, what do you know? You're nothing but an old grandma!"

Finally, I couldn't believe it! After all of these years, here was the moment I longed for. A golden opportunity to pass a like kindness.

My mind raced back to another heavy moment in time. It was two o'clock in the morning. Final rehearsal. My husband Jerry and I were part of a musical group that was the highlight of an international convention. Arriving by plane only that afternoon, we had begun rehearsal shortly following check in at our hotel.

Jerry and I were among a number who had not yet completely unpacked. After hours of rehearsing our choreography routine, the group was fatigued and suffered from jet lag. Nerves were on edge.

Our director was under pressure and short on patience. I had difficulty in perfecting certain steps in a particular medley. My musical partner and I had to repeat the routine a number of times as the group watched. I was exhausted. My mind was foggy, legs sluggish and my feet uncooperative. "Kitty, you are supposed to traipse lightly. You look like a plow horse!" the director bellowed angrily.

Suddenly time stood still as the stage fell silent. The director had often yelled at others in the group but never at me. I am one of those individuals who when yelled at will cry or leave. You may correct me with well-chosen words for I understand the King's English, but don't yell at me.

This group, too, had held its collective breath. All eyes focused on me. Hot tears fought to spill from my eyes, but my fear of humiliation held them at bay. I was frozen in place with indecision. Every fiber in me wanted to run off the stage. "This is it! I've had enough, I don't have to take this. I'm out of here!" I screamed inwardly. But I didn't move. I had a taste of how long eternity must feel.

I vacillated between thoughts of self-preservation and loyalty. How could I let the group down? We were to be back on stage in four hours costumed, energetic and smiling, ready for a breakfast kickoff production. Help, Lord, what do I do?

Suddenly, from the far side of the stage a jovial voice boomed out. "That's okay, baby, you can plow in my field any time!" The room erupted with laughter. The tension broke. We completed the number and only hours later performed on schedule, with my perfectly-executed steps.

Bless Bob, he saved the day! He was one handsome baritone in whose debt I would be forever. Yet, I knew that we rarely have the opportunity to repay a kindness to its original donor. I could only treasure that timely rescue in my heart and pray for an opportunity to pass on his kindness to another. And here it was.

Stepping forward, I placed my arm through Lisa's and announced loudly, "That's okay, sweetheart. There are millions of us grandmothers who would give our false eye teeth to look as good as you do!"

After the laughter subsided, Lisa flashed a grateful smile that let me know my debt had been paid in full.

Kitty Chappell is an Internationally acclaimed speaker and award-winning author of two books, I Can Forgive if I Want to (formerly released as Sins of a Father, Forgiving the Unforgivable) *and* Good Mews, Inspurrrational Stories for Cat Lovers. *Kitty lives in Chandler, Arizona. Visit her website: www. kittychappell.com.*

Delaying What We Truly Deserve
By Paul Ryan

I had a deadline to write a chapter on happiness for this book. I was given notice to do it months ago , but now it is the day before the deadline and I have waited until the last minute to do it. It's the perfect metaphor on how we humans tend to "delay happiness," and yet it is our divine birthright.

Here's a glimpse from my particular journey. When I grew up as a child in Philadelphia, I felt like I went through somewhat of a gray period. Yes, I enjoyed playing sports every day and being a curious young child about the many aspects of life; however I wasn't happy in my heart, because I didn't know what was available to me. Part of it was because my eating habits contributed to me being somewhat unconscious. My life was about quick-fix gratification. Looking back, I ate sugar freely, dairy foods, different types of meat, and various kinds of soda. I had been sold the wrong bill of goods and it was called eating from the four food groups, which I now call "the food groups of unconscious eating."

I moved to England when I was fifteen and went on yet another road of unhealthy eating and subsequently added alcohol and cigarettes. To me it's hard to be happy if your well-being is unbalanced and your food intake is poorly chosen. When I was 17, I found out I had a duodenal ulcer and that was because I had inwardly absorbed the struggles of family bickering and worrying, coupled again with lousy eating habits. Around that time I heard the phrase, "You could live life on a natural high." That is what changed my life.

I went to live on a Kibbutz for two and a half months in the beautiful country of Israel. I was 19 and never felt freer in my life because happiness came through me from being in touch with my new found inner freedom and experiencing a magnificent and beautiful environment. No question about it I was really happy there because I had gotten away from all that I knew before.

173

When I moved to Los Angeles to go to college and pursue acting I went on a journey that would lead me to permanent happiness, because that's exactly where I implemented and committed to "Choosing to live life on a natural high"and knowing it was a total inside job. My first step was getting initiated into Transcendental Meditation. The ceremony was beautiful and I brought flowers, a piece of fruit, and a new white handkerchief to the ceremony. At that time the fee was a mere $75. That $75 was the greatest gift I ever bought myself, because over 20 years later it has brought me so much happiness. The first year and a half were very challenging, because I went through a lot of un-stressing, or as some may say, "purifying the nervous system." I was cleaning out all the stuff that I had put in me and it's hard to move into happiness until you clean the drains of your history and that means emotionally, physically, spiritually, and mentally.

The nervous system is your central pipe line and meditation done twice daily for twenty minutes empties out the rivers of your past and gets you ready for swimming in the ocean of love. Usually one state of mind will lead you to another and Meditation led to me eating on a higher vibration and onto the Arnold Ehret Mucous less Diet. No dairy, no sugar, no meat, and instead choosing to make fresh carrot and celery juices three times a day, and eat lettuce leaves, raw almonds, and salads. My juicer was my new best friend.

I drove almost three hours periodically to Carlsbad, California to have iridology tests with Dr. Benesh, a naturopath, to see what was going on in my internal organs. I was well on my way to happiness, because I chose unequivocally the inner journey. I knew I was never going back because once your health and well being is balanced, you can never return to the unconscious ways of living. My way will be different than yours, but seeing the vision before I took the actions was extremely helpful to me on my road to happiness.

What took me to my next spiritual level was my journey with the Agape International Spiritual Center in Culver City, California. An interesting thing has happened to me twice. The first time I went to a Transcendental Meditation meeting, something didn't click with me. One year later, I was all over it. The first time I went to Agape, I thought it was uplifting, but I wasn't ready to dive in yet. One year later, I went into the deep end and haven't come out yet. I became a spiritual practitioner and go every week to their services. It has definitely taken me to a higher frequency, which has allowed me to deepen and anchor my joy. Joy is something that is a result of you going deeper within yourself and remembering the fullness of who you are.

Speaking for myself, and I believe many others, we can have the tendency to feel happiness comes when you find that certain somebody. And that can happen. But I wouldn't want to depend on another person to fill me up. Sometimes a person comes into our life for a reason, a season, or a lifetime. Trying to hold on to someone else because you've been casting your life partner doesn't always work. They might be holding you back and vise versa. When two people come together to support each other's greatness, it's a beautiful thing. I wish it for everybody. But happiness for each individual on the planet is our own responsibility. I learned along my path that surrendering is the key. We are so used to doing and being in action that we leave out the opportunity of spirit leading the way. I was always led to learning from people who could inspire my growth and continue to do that. If I go to a place where the vibration isn't high or makes me feel uncomfortable, I'm out of there. I'm selfish in this regard, but I think it is necessary. Thinking of nurturing oneself or being nurtured by another who lifts my spirit or matches my vibration is a testament to being wise and intuitive.

Loving self, loving the presence, sending love to others, loving and learning from nature is a great formula for happiness. When the student is ready, the teacher appears. One must be awake and aware to hear the call. If you're ready don't delay. It's your life, it's a gift, and whatever you do, cherish it always.

Paul Ryan produces the series, A BraveHeart View. *He emceed/ produced* The 2009 BraveHeart Awards, *with Maya Angelou and Carol Channing, and is producing The 2010* BraveHeart Awards *with Marianne Williamson in place to be a recipient. Paul was a correspondent for* Entertainment Tonight; *series co-host for* Mid-Morning L.A, *host/producer/owner of 675 in-depth TV Celebrity TV Talk Shows with a "Who's Who of Hollywood." He recently co-starred on* Desperate Housewives, *and is in the upcoming show,* Feel Good TV. *Paul's new Random House book is* The Art of Comedy: Getting Serious about Being Funny. *He has ongoing TV Hosting and Media Coaching Intensives. Visit his website: www.paulryanproductions.com.*

Finding Happiness
By Christine Lynne

Seeking happiness outside ourselves is forever fleeting; Happiness is an "inside job".

I used to love to go shopping all the time and I filled up my life with stuff. Lots of stuff. Stuff that made me happy, but only momentarily. Unconsciously, I became quite the collector of art, books, music, fine crystal, furniture, jewelry, clothes, hats, whimsical toys, knick-knacks, you name it.

Almost as soon as I obtained it, I forgot about it. I didn't even see it in my home anymore; although it was still there, it wasn't hidden away. It was all around me. The place looked like a museum and all the stuff was taking over my life!

Cleverly, I tricked myself into thinking I was so creative to be able to fit all these collections together, but I was running out of space; wall space, floor space, surface space.

I was beginning to feel like all this stuff was smothering me and bogging me down.

Then I came to the realization that all the stuff I was filling my life with was just a "placebo" treatment to try to fill up some emptiness I felt inside.

Now I'm finally getting wise to this, getting in touch with my feelings and living more consciously. I started deconstructing my life, purging, clearing and cleaning out my life. It feels good like a renewal, opening up space for something new to come into my life…

NEWSFLASH! It's the post-consumer era. Simplify. It's time to look within for that's where we'll find true happiness, contentment and peace. It's inside all of us. It's a state of mind. Go within. Quiet the mind. Meditate. We all have a choice to be happy. Believe it or not, it's up to you. Happiness is optional and it's FREE!!!

Happiness Awaits You!

Christine Lynne is a reformed shopaholic and lives in Los Angeles with her beloved Doxie, Gaspar, where they take long walks in Griffith Park. She is a screenwriter-producer, currently working on her passion project, Goddess, *an epic love story set in the Golden Age of Hollywood. Christine is also a LightWorker, using Reiki energy and other modalities for healing and rejuvenation. E-mail Christine through* Goddess Productions: *Xine30@aol. com.*

Finding Joy in the Most Unexpected Place
By Liisa Kyle

For the past decade people have cajoled me to join the social networking site Facebook. I resisted mightily. Once a month or so, I'd receive invitations from various people, both professional contacts and social acquaintances, asking me to 'friend' them on Facebook. "Thanks but no thanks," I'd reply, a bit smugly. "I'm proudly Facebook-free."

A month ago, the book project closest to my heart, the one I knew was a sure-fire winner, got axed. This project had been so dear to me, its sudden and unexpected demise made me feel lousy. It didn't help that my creative partner on the project proceeded to disparage my work to our agent, his mailing list and passersby.

I was lower than low; listless and self-deprecating. It didn't matter that I'm well versed in myriad methods of manifesting happiness in one's daily life. My brain may know better but my spirit insisted on doing the opposite. To make matters worse, events conspired, several other work projects collided and suddenly I was forced to establish a profile on, you guessed it, Facebook.

Gritting my teeth, terror in my heart, I embarked on my new life on a social networking website. Little did I realize that Facebook would be my salvation. To my astonishment, Facebook was the catalyst to generating much daily joy in my life.

By that afternoon I was animated, delighted and comfortably ensconced amid a supportive network of friends and colleagues. My head was spinning, my heart was singing and I was happy.

It turns out that one of the primary tasks of getting started on Facebook is to find 'friends'. They may be real, true buddies. They might be social acquaintances or work associates. It doesn't matter. Any consensual contact is counted as a 'friend' in the Facebook universe. You locate someone you know, send them a 'friend request' and wait for them to 'confirm' or 'ignore' you.

It seemed odd to send out messages ("Will you be my friend?") as if I was back in elementary school, but apparently that's what one does. In my case, the response was immediate and unexpectedly gratifying. Suddenly, friend confirmations clogged up my profile page. My 'friend count' rose as my message box filled with warm words of welcome from folks eager to reconnect.

Tickled by each successful contact, I was motivated to find more. To my surprise, I felt compelled to revisit each chapter of my life, even the 'icky' periods I had always tried to expunge from my memory. Rather than bemoaning the pain of those periods, I looked past the muck seeking human gems my favorite people during difficult times. Sure grad school was a toxic place, but there were some lovely folks there, hidden among the academic vampires. What a pleasure to reach out and find them now, in happier times.

Even excellent chapters were worth plumbing for lost relationships, once cherished. The two happiest years of my life were those I lived in Vancouver, Canada. Sure, I'm in touch with some of my pals from that period, but I'd lost contact with others, somehow. Going through my old address books and email lists, I was able to use Facebook to reinstate friendships that had slipped away.

The exercise was also a way of refreshing professional contacts I thought had withered away years ago. I started to feel better about perceived missed opportunities in the past. Perhaps there was hope for some of the manuscripts languishing in my drawer, after all.

I was astonished at the number of folks who had drifted out of my life over time and how easy it was to reconnect with them, using "Hi, I'm getting started on Facebook" as my excuse. Even if someone was not on Facebook, my 'friend-finding' enterprise sparked offline reconnections via phone and email.

How fun it was to catch up! How uplifting to learn of the beautiful lives that people had created and how touching to commiserate over challenges they had faced. These friendly exchanges put an immediate stop to any further wallowing on my part. How could I be grumpy in the midst of so many friends?

How delightful to have conversations evolve in new ways: It was odd to be discussing dog obedience issues with a writer whose work I'd long admired, for example. It was surreal to be chatting about motorcycle maintenance with the person who had been the star trumpeter in our high school band. (I had been but a mediocre clarinetist and if we ever did actually speak during high school, it was no doubt limited to shouting "Catch!" as we unloaded twenty pound boxes of "Texas Citrus Fruit" off an eighteen wheeler to stack them for our band trip fundraising sale). Now, thanks to unexpected email and Facebook conversations, every day held some engaging exchanges to brighten my day.

Then there was the external validation. Apparently, from the perspective of an outsider, my life looks pretty interesting. ("Oh, that's right. I guess I have worked on four continents. Come to think of it, I've visited fifty-plus countries. I'm well published and my metal, ceramic and fused glass pieces have indeed been in bona fide exhibits. My husband has, in fact, supported my creative endeavors enthusiastically for seventeen years. I guess I'm not a complete loser after all.") By highlighting my adventures and accomplishments, my 'Facebook friends' put the demise of my recent project into vivid perspective. It was but a blip on my unique path.

More than just reconnecting people, the Facebook platform makes us a part of each other's lives. I hadn't realized how isolated I'd been before. Now, by intermittently monitoring the 'Live Feed' that chronicles the postings of my friends, I'm instantly aware of their triumphs, witticisms and foibles. I can send immediate congratulations, bandy about some catch phrases or offer words of encouragement. I can phone when they send up a flare.

Although I set about the task rather clumsily and haphazardly, essentially what I was doing was gathering my tribe. As our connections have re-established and deepened, I'm increasingly aware of the oneness of our lives. I feel more loved and more loving, as if cocooned in affection. In that space, it's very difficult to be down in the dumps on any given day.

I am not advocating Facebook as a catalyst for happiness. It was in my case, but for you it's apt to be a completely different trigger.

The point is that, even in the depths of despair, it is possible to find happiness. It doesn't seem like it at the time, I know. When you're down, really down, there's a tendency to believe you are doomed to be unhappy forever. But it's not true.

You can be happy. There are scientifically proven techniques to change how you're feeling. You just need to find the right catalyst for you to connect with your own true, authentic happiness; that joy that's deep down; that kernel of 'self' that feels right. For some people that might mean professional counseling. For others it might require finding an outlet for a fervent but unexpressed passion. Some folks may blossom through giving service to the community. Others may rely on advice from self-help books. Some people may simply choose to be happy from this point on, and act accordingly. There is no one formula that works for everyone. You have to find what's right for you.

One final point: Note the irony in my story. The very thing I resisted the most is the thing that pulled me back from the brink. Much as I'm embarrassed to admit it, Facebook has made me happier, in a real and profound way. My happiness set point is considerably higher today than it was a few months ago, mostly because of my daily interactions with my Facebook tribe. So, ask yourself: what are you resisting? What is persisting, or repeating in your life, despite all your efforts to avoid it? Perhaps it is the catalyst that will allow you connect with the happiness inside you.

Liisa Kyle is a co-author of this book.

Pathway to Happiness
By Belita Davison

One of my missions in life is to teach my two granddaughters, Brionna, age 5, and Mackenzie, age 7, how to find the pathway to happiness at an early age. This would include learning the joy of loving and sharing, the knowledge of the power of forgiveness and instilling in them a zest for life with the confidence that they can do anything.

To my heart's delight, I have been blessed to have been an integral part of their lives from birth, and we now have an unshakeable bond. I remember when we were getting ready to move from Sitka, Alaska and were planning a two week road trip. My daughter was dreading being in a car everyday with kids who were 2 and 4. We walked out that first morning, flew to Seattle and picked up the car we had barged down from the island.

"I looked at the kids and said, "Hooray! It's the Fun Machine."

That whole two weeks, they couldn't wait to climb aboard the Fun Machine to see what new adventure awaited us that day. My daughter, Brite, would look at me and just laugh at how naming the car had changed everyone's outlook about the trip. Needless to say, we had an absolute blast on our travels that summer.

One of the things that can bring the greatest joy in life is sharing the gift of love and friendship with others. When we got to Arizona, we had left 60 degree weather and were hit with 120 degrees of heat. I grabbed the grand babies and told Brite I was taking them to Kingman where I had friends to visit, while we adjusted to the difference in temperature. Brionna and Mackenzie were sad because they didn't have any friends in Kingman and I told them I was going to share all of my girlfriends with them. We had a great visit reconnecting with old friends.

A couple of months later, my high school reunion came up and we went back to Kingman. The girls made sure their mom knew "not too worry," they were going to share all of their new friends with her.

Brionna got out of the car in Kingman and said "Girlfriends, girlfriends where are you? We're here!" Friendship is a gift from God and love is a never ending resource that is free.

The kids started school and I noticed them struggling and coming home with a different countenance than I was used to seeing. We used to wake up together and enjoy the beauty of a brand new sunrise to start the day, and all of a sudden things were changing and I didn't like what I was seeing. I know my grandchildren aren't perfect, but I also understand how the attitudes of others can affect you if you let them. That's when I developed my Bad Attitude Adjustment Dance and named it my "Oh, Happy Day Dance".

Whenever I saw a bad attitude appearing, we would all have to get in a line and dance until we had an attitude adjustment. We used to do it to change our own attitudes, but that is seldom needed now. Now we do it just for fun.

I called the girls to say good morning last week and I asked Brionna if she was having a good day. "Of course I am, Mimi, why wouldn't I be?" she said.

"That's right, baby girl, because we can choose to be happy," I replied. She agreed, saying she chooses to be happy everyday. It took me a long time to realize the power that we possess over our daily lives.

Another philosophy I have tried to instill is that they can do anything they put their minds to. They are not allowed to say "I can't do that". Instead, the proper response is "I can do that, but I just haven't learned how yet". I want them to have the faith that they can accomplish anything with the sky being the limit.

Last, but not least, is the lesson of the power of forgiveness. We pray together before bed time and ask forgiveness for things we may have done wrong, and also lift up those who have wronged us. Harboring anger hurts you more than the person you're mad at. It is also something that can fester out of control and eat away at the heart of you. I believe if people could learn to forgive, that it would filter into every other area of their lives and make things brighter.

My grand babies have such loving hearts. Once they asked me if they were supposed to love everyone.

"Yes," I said.

"Even the bad people?"

"Bad people need us to pray for them more because they need an attitude adjustment and need to learn about love."

With childlike innocence the girls agreed and purposed to love everyone they came in contact with. If only we could take a lesson from our children in how simple life should be.

Belita Davison has lived in Flagstaff, Arizona for the past 2 years. She got divorced 6 years ago, after almost 30 years of marriage. She had been living in Sitka, Alaska for 15 years and went back to school, got her degree and then moved back to Arizona. She has been able to move on without a spirit of bitterness and is grateful that unforgiveness doesn't rule her life. Belita believes she has many things to be thankful for and is blessed beyond measure with loving friends and family.

Hollywood Made Me A Better Daughter
By JC Sullivan

Actors utilize technique breakdown to "become" the characters you see.

Essentially it is an in-depth psychological analysis of who the characters are, their motivations, their challenges and how they view their spot in the world.

I used this same method to improve my relationship with my father. We had a pretty good relationship, but I knew it could be a whole lot better. We fought a lot and as much as I don't want to admit it, I was as stubborn as he. I believed I had disappointed him and nothing I did would ever be good enough. Could I be partly to blame? Were any of my assumptions even true? I had never gone back and adjusted my family "role." I saw my family's story only through my outdated lens, repeating silly childhood patterns. So, I used technique breakdown for a long overdue emotional check-up.

The first step is to analyze the character, which in this case is my Dad. What obstacles had he overcome? What did he really want (a character's "super objective") out of life? Then I wrote my father's back-story, or significant events in his life. I thought about all he went through and developed his view of the world. I marveled in the obstacles he had managed to overcome and wondered if there were things he wished he could have told his parents when they were living. I chose his super objective: a man who wanted to be loved.

I raised the stakes, pretending that this would be the last chance I had to talk to my Father. I wasn't ready to improv one of the most important scenes of my life, so I wrote him a one-page thank you letter, making it as specific as possible. Specificity makes it truly unique. I rewrote and rewrote, sure to include the wonderful things that he had done for me. I had forgotten so many of his sacrifices.

Why was I picking fights with this man? I really appreciated my Dad. Writing this letter was so helpful that I wrote one for my

Mom, too. Particularly in emotionally-charged situations, letters enable you to gather your thoughts and they can be reread by the recipient.

My stage directions were to act the opposite of the way I had been acting for all these years, to act as if they were the most proud, loving parents in the world in utter amazement of my life. Treat them like your best friends. I was embarrassed to realize I wouldn't treat an enemy the way I had been treating my parents. I went home and really listened. I saw my filter in action. I had viewed everything as if through a lens that my parents were criticizing me. By changing the lens, your reaction changes. With this new adult lens, I actually heard what my parents were saying. They told great stories and made me laugh. Not being stuck in our previous family roles, we had a fun dinner, as adults.

The next day, I handed my thank you letter to my Dad and told him I wanted to tell him he was a great Dad. He looked surprised and said he'd read it later. I went downstairs and handed my Mom her letter who read it right in front of me. It led to one of our best conversations.

All these years, she was harboring fears and regrets of how she raised me and thought I hated her. Both of us had been operating under completely false assumptions.

As wonderful as my time with my Mom was, I agonized. Had my father read his letter and was choosing to ignore me? Did he care? Old habits die hard. The "old me" came roaring out and believed he was deliberately torturing me. My new choice said, "Wait, be loving." Then I realized I couldn't change my Dad. But I could change the way I dealt with him.

I also remembered his back-story. His generation wasn't raised to discuss emotions, nor were they given tools to do so. I was being demanding, a petulant child, to request him to make such a big leap on my time frame and on my terms. Then, an even more superior choice surfaced, trust that everything's fine. I did what I needed to do. It's not about approval and acceptance. While that would be nice, do what you believe in your heart to be right and let go. We can't change others, but we control how we view them. I really love my Father and vowed to stop fighting with him, particularly on the insignificant points.

So, I let it all go and kept on being my "new" daughter, an adult secure in her parents' love, who enjoys spending time with them. With such an optimistic view of my parents, and still believing I would try and treat them like my best friends, I showed them a DVD of a storytelling event I had done. I told them how great actors and storytellers make it look so easy that we all think we can do it, so please, be kind. I was still new to acting, working on getting better.

My mother loved it. My Dad laughed. They told me how much they admired my courage and couldn't believe I wrote stories and told them (without the use of notes). It meant the world to me.

As I was leaving, my stoic father looked at me and said, "I appreciate the letter."

I replied, "I meant it. You're a great Dad. Thanks!"

This was a huge step in a much better relationship. Sad that so much pain could've been solved years ago if I had just bothered to try a different tactic.

When I called home, I found myself really wanting to hear their voices on the other end of the phone. My mother said that she and my father had been talking and how much they loved my visit. Of all the gifts that I had ever given them, my DVD was their favorite. It had helped them feel like they were part of my world. And they looked forward to seeing others.

Who would have ever thought that acting class would teach me to be a better person?

JC Sullivan, a poet and writer is a proud member of the Travelers Century Club (www.travelerscenturyclub.org) for people who have been to more than 100 countries. She has financed all her own travels. Having worked in virtually every industry, she now tries to avoid the cubicle at all costs. Currently she is searching for her inner Latina and living in Mendoza, Argentina. E-mail her at: jobfreejennifer@yahoo.com.

STEPPING STONES

Meditation is a time-honored technique proven to increase happiness, reduce stress, enhance physical health, improve psychological functioning and to heal mind and body. It can lower blood pressure, alleviate depression and anxiety, reduce pain, bolster the immune system, increase concentration and more.

The basic concept is to devote some time to quieting your mind.

There is no wrong way to meditate. Whatever happens is fine. If you are new to meditation, you may find that your 'monkey mind' jumps around a fair bit. This is natural. Whenever you notice a flurry of thoughts, gently bring your attention back to your meditation.

According to Tibetan master Yongey Mingyur Rinpoche, it's better to aim for more frequent, short sessions of three to five minutes duration than to attempt fewer, longer sessions.

Below is an assortment of meditation techniques. Try one technique for a week. See how it goes. Then try another for the next week. Over time, you'll find out what works best for you.

Meditation Options:

1. Focus on the breath. Simply sit quietly and pay attention to your breathing. When your attention drifts, bring it back to your breathing.

2. Select a word to repeat to yourself (e.g. 'peace' or 'love' or 'joy' or 'ohm'). When your attention drifts, bring it back to your focus word.

3. Select an image on which to concentrate. This might be a visual image from a pleasant memory

or it might be an actual photo or painting you have in front of you.

4.   Focus your attention on an object such as a candle.

5.   Try to simply clear your mind completely. As thoughts arise, label them as 'thinking thinking' or 'judging judging' or 'obsessing obsessing' and allow them to pass by like clouds pass through the sky.

6.   Ask 'What do I need to know?" Quiet your mind and listen attentively for an answer.

7.   Mindful eating. Use a grape or a raisin or any small, healthful item. Look at it. Really look at its texture and appearance. Smell it. Roll it between your fingers–what does it feel like? Does touching it make a sound? Now lick the item. What do your taste buds reveal? Hold the item in your mouth. Roll it around. Feel it touching your teeth. Bite down. Let the flavor wash over your tongue. Chew slowly and purposefully. Swallow and focus on the residual taste in your mouth.

8.   Purposeful action. Pick an activity, any activity. It might be washing the dishes or folding laundry or petting your cat. Whatever it is, do it slowly and with the utmost attention. Engage all your senses and really focus on being there, in the moment.

9.   Walking mediation. As you step forward, slowly and with purpose, focus your attention on your motion. Feel the air against your body as you move.

10. Body scan. Lie down in a comfortable position. Now put all your attention on your left toes. When you're ready, shift your attention to the middle of that foot. Then to your left heel. Move your attention to your left ankle and, taking your time, shift it to your left calf, then knee, then thigh then hip. Repeat the process using your right leg. Move up from the hips and pelvis, putting your attention on your abdomen, your internal organs, your ribcage, your heart, your shoulders and, eventually your throat. Scan your arms, one at a time. Shift your attention to every aspect of your head and face.

11. Time in nature. Find a place outdoors to sit. Fill your senses with the sights, sounds, smells and sensations of that place.

There are many CDs available that will walk you through a guided meditation. You can find them at your library or on the internet.

CHAPTER 9

Acceptance

I don't believe it. I have bills to pay, emails to answer, and right now my internet is down. I keep getting those inane little boxes that tell me to diagnose the problem and all they come up with after ten minutes is that a cable is unplugged even though I've checked every cable about fifteen times. Frustrated. Yes. Do I want to scream? YES. What happened to that glorious calm feeling I had when I woke up merely an hour ago? Gone, out the window. Not a trace of it left. Yes, I want to scream.

Does the above paragraph ring a bell of familiarity? Sometimes it's the little things, the itty bitty little things that should not matter that get to us the most. Maybe for you it's rush hour traffic and there's a car that knows you want to change lanes, your turn signal has been blinking forever, and of course you're late for your appointment. If you can't move over and get off this blasted freeway you might have to drive another five miles out of your way and be even later. Yikes. It can make you want to scream.

Besides moving to Timbuktu, what can you do? Right now, just reading this, you may be feeling a little like screaming. Breathe. Just stop and tell yourself to take three deep, deep, deep, breaths and hold each one a few seconds in your lungs. Exhale slowly, slowly, letting it all out, giving it all over to God, your angels, guides, or Source. Ask them to take care of the little, and big situations that you are facing. Breathe again and again. Try this while placed on hold for the eighth time in a row, or when you're stalled at a traffic light. Picture your tension melting away.

Remember that the screaming usually doesn't work. Although you may have tried it a few more times than you would care to admit. What is the key to unlocking the door that holds all of your answers whether for life changing events or being placed on hold?

Acceptance.

Going Home Again
By Maggie TerryViale

Two weeks in the ideal climate of California! I could feel the gentle moisture of the bay on my face mingle with the hazy sun as I gazed at the rolling hills dotted with majestic oaks. Here and there a vineyard graced a hillside with a celebration of crimson and yellow leaves still clinging to the vines that had just been harvested.

I wanted so to move back to the place where I was raised, but the timing wasn't right. I boarded my flight back to Phoenix. When I walked out of the airport I was confronted with oven-like temperatures in the bone-dry, desert city choking in smog. In short, I came back kicking and screaming. I did not want to live here. I had spent almost twenty years in Arizona, most of them wonderful, but my time was up, I told God.

But God didn't think so. There was more for me still in Phoenix. I could have rebelled and gone against my Guidance and moved back to California, but I knew in my heart, for some unknown reason, the timing was not right. Ok. Fine. All right. I'll stay. Yes, there were a few grumbles, but as soon as I agreed to stay, everything shifted.

I fell right into my writing, my circle of friends, and my artwork. I gazed appreciatively at the hummingbirds of joy that hovered outside my window. I saw sunsets that looked like an orb of gold setting the clouds on fire; breathtaking! Even unexpected money flowed in. And the key to my attitude adjustment and appreciation of this desert paradise? Acceptance.

Maggie TerryViale is a co-author of this book.

God Sends a Messenger
By Neva Howell

It was September 13, 2001, just two days after the horrific events of 9/11. I was sitting at the kitchen table. Across from me was my partner, with whom I shared a monogamous relationship we both considered a spiritual marriage for the past seven years. I had just learned he had been intimate with another woman.

It was so normal, I couldn't believe it. Sitting at the dining room table, the way we had for thousands of mornings over the years, it took a moment for reality to shift. It was so normal, that moment when my world shattered. I heard a half-laugh jump from my throat. I sat stunned. I did not believe it.

I heard what he said. I just simply could not believe it. Then, I believed.

Just two days after September 11, sitting there in the normal kitchen table, I had a vision of myself as one of the towers, crumbling to dust. It was over. I was over. Ground Zero.

Impotent rage followed, and then despair so deep that I felt it in my bone marrow.

I lay myself down to die. If this was not my life, this that I had lived for the past seven years, then none else would be my life.

I was not suicidal. I did not have that much energy. I just lay down.

The first words out of my mouth, when finally I could speak were, "I have to leave."

Yet, I could not leave. For days, I just cried. I lay in the bed and cried. Who was this woman, crumbled and demolished? I didn't recognize her as me. In fact, I would never have thought that the end of any relationship could have devastated me to this degree.

In the midst of this soul-level devastation, I got a phone call out of the blue from a friend I had not talked to for months. Looking back on it now, I know it was a God Send.

I told her what was going on and she listened with compassion. I wept more when I thought there could be no more tears. I told her I didn't know how I could find the strength to leave. There was a pause on the other end of the phone and then, a reply I neither expected nor understood. She said simply, "I think I'll clean out my closet."

My first reaction was anger. Why was she talking about closets when my life was falling apart around me? Then, even more oddly, she repeated it, "I think I'll clean out my closet." In some sort of telekinetic wave, I got it. I saw what she was giving me. I looked over to the closet in my office, and felt something shift in me. She then said that whenever she had a task that was too overwhelming, like cleaning the house, she would start with something that would not overwhelm.

That day, I cleaned out my closet. Then, I packed a box, then another, then another. And I left.

What I discovered, as I cleaned out each little corner of our space together, is that I began to retrieve parts of myself. It happened as I chose what to keep, what to leave, and what to throw away or donate. I threw away a lot. I donated a lot. And what I ended up taking, mattered to me.

So, if you find yourself realizing that you have to leave, but feel unable to do it, start with something small. Clean out your closet.

Neva Howell's bio follows her story in Chapter 5.

Opening To Your Lit Up Path
By Judith
A Peace of the Universe

Spirit I am ready for my next most lit up Path.

I am paying attention.

I would like chills up my spine,

my heart to blast singing

when I am on my right clear path

with grace and ease in quick earth time.

You will find Judith at A Peace of the Universe, *a spiritual bookstore, a space to embrace you for all that you are. The bookstore was given to Judith by Spirit over 17 years ago. Please visit the website for this complete story: www. APeaceoftheUniverse.com or come by for a free hug from Judith at 7000 E. Shea Blvd. Suite 1710, Scottsdale, AZ 85254*

Breathe Between the Lines
By Trisha Koury-Stoops

Have you ever noticed the lighting in the grocery stores? I mean seriously, who looks good in florescent! I make a list but I always get distracted. The aisles feel so narrow, like I'm shopping in coach on an airplane or stuck in aisle seven in bumper-to-bumper traffic with an uncontrollable cart that swerves back and forth. To make matters worse, people are staring at me like I am drunk as I keep crashing into them. "Excuse me," I say with a half cracked smile as I am having trouble breathing because the aisles are moving closer together. *I've got to get out of this aisle. Oh my god, this woman is blocking me. Get off the phone! What was she thinking when she left the house this morning.*

"Stop It!" I mumble out loud. "What is going on? I'm not a bitch! Is there no air in this place?"

Are you with me so far? Now, the fun part really begins. My chest feels really tight. My hands and face are tingling and the palms become sweaty. I feel like there is Saran Wrap over my head. I can see people talking but I can't hear or understand what they are saying. To make matters worse, I think my brain is crawling out from my ears. I think I am having a heart attack! I don't want to die!

Sound familiar? Then welcome to the growing VIP Club of Anxiety and Panic! Wondering why I call it that? Because when I discovered it was only the intelligent, overachievers who find themselves with this oxygen-deprived, jumbled brain, out of control disorder, then I was able to laugh. I'm smart and crazy! Great! First of all, we all take ourselves too seriously. We push and push wanting something so bad that it drives us crazy, literally. And when you get close to reaching your goals you panic! When I was able to find humor in my madness this was the unfolding of the first blessing, which started a path of release and acceptance. That is something, somewhere along the way I had lost.

The second blessing was learning to face the boogieman. Remember when you were a kid and you slept with a night-light? After all, there where monsters in the closet and under your bed, right? Now you've reached an age where you should be able to sleep in the dark but somehow the monsters have returned! You hear them plotting against you. You want to get out of bed and turn on the light to see if they are really there but you are too afraid to get out of the bed in case they are real. I finally mustered up some courage and reached out, grabbing the boogieman by the throat and pulling him out into the light only to discover it was me who was hiding under the bed. I have found that in cleaning out your closets you discover the important treasures that have been waiting to be found.

The third and final blessing through anxiety is the art of listening to yourself and reconnecting to the spiritual side. In other words, get out of the wind tunnel. I went to a place called Universal City here in Southern California. It's like a little entertainment city that sits on top of a hill, overlooking Hollywood. It's a great place to be outside, see a movie, eat or listen to a live band. As I was walking around I came upon a very large glass tube, which sat in the middle of the plaza.

I suddenly stopped and watched with amazement as this young girl, about 12 years old, put on this flight suit and gear. I first thought this was a Hollywood stunt demonstration about to start until I noticed a number of kids and adults waiting in line. When she stepped in, the door shutting behind her, she stood tall and brave and gave the controller the thumbs up.

Suddenly this powerful wind began to blow, lunging her straight to the top. She soon held out her arms and was flying. She then began turning and doing tricks. She had no fear. It was a controlled simulation of jumping out of a plane and flying. Watching her, I was amazed on how in control she was.

Then a guy got in; he was about mid twenties. He seemed confident and a bit cocky, but following the young girl was not an easy thing to do. He really needed someone experienced with him. I laughed as he flailed around like a rag doll with his eyes wide with fear. It was then I realized I was just like that guy appearing confident as I step into wind tunnel after wind tunnel, flailing around like a rag doll, trapped, fearful and unable to find my way out.

Before the anxiety, I used to be free, confident, fearless and centered. "I want my inner girl back," I said to myself. So I got back into my spiritual place, listened for my inner voice to guide me. I realized that gifts would come when they are meant to and the rest was not important. I am now relearning the art of finding my flight path and that is empowering!

Trisha Koury-Stoops has always had a passion for writing. She has written for film and television. She has also written articles, blogs and speeches for political, sports and charity events. Trisha is featured in the spotlight A-List Alumni for Writers Boot Camp and a member of Academy of Television Arts & Science. E-mail her at: kwannawrite@earthlink.net.

The Joy of Food
By Gwen Kenneally

Life is like one great big meal. The more tasty bites you take the more delicious it is.

Food is my passion, my love and my joy. I eat for pleasure. I find great creativity and excitement in my work. I have never been one to play it safe in the kitchen and I have never met a food challenge I have not been willing to take head on.

Being a chef and a food writer I get into interesting conversations around my relationship with food. Because of the pressure I can put on myself for perfection and the media frenzy, sometimes I start to feel 'not so great' about myself. I remember looking in the mirror one day. All I saw was rolls of fat and imperfection. I burst into tears just hating what I saw. I kept repeating "I hate my body, I hate myself." I cried for a while and wondered how to fix it.

I heard a small voice from within gently whispering, "Just love yourself. Love yourself and embrace your curves. Eat for pleasure." The message became so clear to me. It was not about my 'muffin top' or wanting to look a certain way. It was really about self-love and self-acceptance. Being 5 feet 10 inches tall, I think I would look ridiculous as a size 2, but I can step up my exercise and eat a bit lighter. But what is this message about eating for pleasure?

You cannot possibly be eating for pleasure when you are chowing down a couple of quarter pounders on the Los Angeles parking lot known as the 405 freeway. It does not mean making a T.V. date with Ben and Jerry, mac and cheese or Pepperidge Farms.

Mindful preparation and eating for pleasure are when you truly express love through food, love of yourself and those you care about. This means spending time with flavors. It means taking local, seasonal ingredients from the earth and carefully preparing them with the most exotic seasoning. Take risks by being creative with vegetables that you have never tried before.

What about the idea of a simple and mindful meal? It starts with you catching a vision of what your event looks like. Who are you cooking for? What does your table looks like? What is your menu? It is not about throwing a couple of pizzas on the table and ringing a 'come and get it' bell. No, it is about inviting people you care about into your home. It can be simple, very simple, but it is truly about expressing love through food and spending time with friends and family.

I had the gift last summer of being the mom in charge of the garden at my daughter's school. What a better classroom that a massive edible playground and an opportunity to take what is fresh from the garden to the table? I thought I was there to teach cooking to the children, but I just stepped back and allowed them to create. They came up with things I could have never imagined. Can this be the new food trend? Expressing love, time and creativity through food. I hope so.

Here is a recipe through which you can find happiness through the practice of mindful preparation and eating for pleasure. Using 60% cacao (or higher) is a wonderful antioxidant and a little bite can bring so much joy and pleasure.

Assortment of Truffles
2/3 cup whipping cream
2 cups Ghirardelli 60% Cacao Chocolate Chips
1-tablespoon brown rice syrup
1-teaspoon vanilla extract
2 teaspoons Grand Marnier
1/4 cup unsweetened cocoa powder
1 cup sweetened shredded coconut, toasted
1 cup finely chopped hazelnuts

Bring cream to boil in heavy medium saucepan. Remove from heat. Add chocolate; whisk until melted and smooth Add rice syrup. Divide in half. Whisk the vanilla to half and the Grand Marnier to the other. Pour into two medium bowls. Cover; chill until firm, overnight.

Line baking sheet with waxed paper. Drop mixture by rounded teaspoonfuls onto prepared baking sheet. Refrigerate until firm, about three hours

Place cocoa, coconut and nuts in separate bowls. Roll truffles between hands into rounds. Roll 1/3 of truffles in cocoa, 1/3 in coconut and 1/3 in nuts. Cover with plastic; chill until ready to serve.

Gwen Kenneally believes that every meal should be about pleasure and savoring every bite. She started cooking as a young child with family and friends and realized the power of great foods with recipe traditions. She has run the gamut of working with award-winning Chefs in the kitchens of movie stars to creating mouth-watering soups for the homeless during the holidays. A celebrated food writer, she also shares recipes and her passion for food on several TV shows. As a caterer and party planner she is known in the food world for bold, fresh imaginative food. Visit her website: www.mydailyfind.com.

Life's Lemons Lead to Lemon Meringue Pie
By Chellie Campbell

White-faced and trembling, my office manager, Carla, handed me the message that would change my life. Just looking at her, my heart sank. I knew something was terribly wrong. What tragedy had struck that made her look so forlorn?

After building my business management firm over four years, I was flying high. I had just bought out my partners and was going it alone as an entrepreneur. I was on top of the world. Now, horrified and dumb-struck, I read the message Carla handed me and saw my dreams crumble into dust. It was worse than I could have believed possible. Our biggest bread-and-butter client had just cancelled our contract and was pulling out with only two weeks notice. 75% of my income had just walked out our door

What was I going to do? How could I accept such a loss of income? I wished I had never gotten up that morning. I kept reviewing the circumstances and beating myself up: How could I not have known the client was unhappy? Why wasn't I smarter, more mature, aware, convincing?

I mourned for days, of course. Told all my friends my sad story. Wallowed in my pain like the victim I was. Told myself how unfair it all was, how awful the client was, and how virtuous and blameless I was. But I knew there were warning signs I had ignored. Some of the members of the client group had groused about our billings. A new president and a new board of directors were taking over the reins of the organization. An important meeting was held without me. The skies had darkened and the waves were rising, but I didn't reduce sail or batten the hatches. So then I switched targets and started beating myself up instead of mentally pummeling my soon-to-be-ex clients.

Then the still, small voice inside me, said, "Great, Chellie. But crying isn't going to get you where you want to go." I sat up when I heard it. I recognized that voice. My Intuition, my Spirit Guide, my Guardian Angel, my Higher Self, The Voice of Inner

Wisdom—call it what you will. Like E.F. Hutton, when that voice speaks, I listen. And in that moment, I saw that I wasn't doomed and I wasn't dead.

Like a poker player with only a chip and a chair left between winning the tournament and elimination, in that moment, my determination to succeed took over. I didn't have much left, but I wasn't completely broke yet. I had some chips and I had an office chair. My business might be smaller, but it was still a business. I had built it up once and I would just have to do it all over again.

Over the next year I faced huge hurdles and had to negotiate ways over or around them. I had to become very creative in order to survive and enlisted the aid of everyone I knew, family, friends, employees, my banker, my landlords, my clients who stuck with me and all the vendors I couldn't pay in full each month. I renegotiated for smaller office space, lower monthly payments on loans, sold off equipment and furniture. I haunted networking groups, looking for referrals and new clients.

Every day I listened to Robert Schuller's audio tape *Tough Times Never Last—Tough People Do* about people overcoming tragedies—and said to myself, if they can do it, I can too. I posted a sign that read "EGBOK" (Everything's Gonna Be OK) over my desk, and then got busy. I learned how to make more money, to keep a light touch, to give to others even when I didn't think I had anything to give. And in the process, I grew spiritually, too, finding a new strength, serenity, stability and self-esteem.

This was also the year, 1989, that the recession hit California full-force. The economy spiraled downward and everyone was suffering. Many people had heard my story, that I had weathered a huge crisis in my business and personal life, and asked me to meet with them to tell them how I did it. How was I able to survive? How was I able to keep smiling while I struggled? What were the financial techniques I used to cut my budget, and then expand again as business grew? How did I combine a wealthy material life with a wealthy spiritual life?

I started counseling clients over lunch. Three people in the same week told me, "You should be teaching this!" I have learned to listen when I get the same message from three people who don't know each other. It's always my Higher Power trying to get my attention. So I started putting material together for a seminar.

I taught my first "Financial Stress Reduction® Workshop" in February of 1990. It was successful and fun, so I taught another one. And another. Finally, I realized this work made my whole life make sense. My performance skills from the years I spent as a professional actress combined with my financial skills allowed me to create a workshop that was both entertaining and produced great results for my clients.

I saw that every life experience I had been through had been training me for this. With that realization, I sold the business management company and jumped into teaching workshops full-time. Now I have a business I love, work that doesn't feel hard, clients who praise me and pay me. My first book was published, and then my second one, too. I started licensing others as Financial Stress Reduction® Coaches and my telecourses have participants from all over the world learning to master their money and create the life of their dreams. I have wonderful relationships with my family and friends, and I'm making more money and having more fun than ever before in my life.

It's been years since that awful day when I thought my life was over. But it had actually just begun. What looked like the biggest loss of my life was actually the biggest gift. What looked like bad news, once I accepted and changed my attitude was really good news. The door that closed was just guiding me to a bigger door, a better door, a richer door. Now I thank God that client left me! Without their lemons, I might never have learned to bake lemon meringue pie.

Chellie Campbell is the creator of the popular Financial Stress Reduction® Workshops now taught by certified trainers throughout the country. The author of The Wealthy Spirit *and* Zero to Zillionaire, *she is one of Marci Shimoff's "Happy 100" in her NYT bestseller* Happy for No Reason *and contributed stories to Jack Canfield's recent books* You've Got to Read This Book! *and* Life Lessons from Chicken Soup for the Soul. *She is prominently quoted as a financial expert in The Los Angeles Times, Pink, Good Housekeeping, Lifetime, Essence, Woman's World and more than 50 popular books. For* 30 Days to a Wealthy Spirit, *daily inspirational emails and other information, Visit her website:* www.Chellie.com *or E-mail her at* Chellie@Chellie.com

STEPPING STONES

The serenity prayer invites us to 'accept the things we cannot change'.

Activity: Think about an unpleasant event in your life, something that you feel was not your fault and over which you had no control.

How did you react? In particular, what did you do to try to change the situation?

_____

_____

_____

_____

What were the consequences of your actions?

_____

_____

_____

_____

Now, imagine that, instead of fighting things or trying to control what was going on , you accepted the situation. How would that have changed your experience?

_____

_____

_____

_____

What constructive actions you can take to improve the situation?

_____

_____

_____

_____

Remember the first and most important part of the Serenity Prayer:

> God grant me the serenity
> to accept the things I cannot change;
> courage to change the things I can;
> and wisdom to know the difference.

CHAPTER 10

Recovering from Loss

Losing a loved one is devastating and often debilitating. Everyone handles grief in a different way. No one comes through it unchanged. Sometimes people feel that a a part of them has been taken away. The challenge is to go on with their lives, continuing their own journey, following the new path that they have been forced to follow.

Granted you will not be happy in the same way you were when the physical presence of your loved ones walked beside you, but you can be happy by reaching out for life and remembering that you are never alone.

One of the most beautiful stories told about the tragedy of 9/11 was about a disabled man who was unable to leave the tower because he was confined to a wheel chair. He had a friend and co-worker who sacrificed his own life so that his disabled friend would not be trapped in the burning building by himself and die alone. Life is unpredictable; love is the courage that enables us to rise above the pain and suffering and become heroes.

Remember that the loved ones who have gone before us are really not out of reach or touch. Open your heart and mind to the signs and messages that assure you that love is eternal. It can never be lost. It is always there if you believe in it and open yourself up to its healing power.

Rob's Tree
By Sam Turner

In 1959 there were three palm trees in our back yard, three small palms and a flower planter at the base of the back wall filled with zinnias. From the north brick wall to the back kitchen door was thirty-five feet of dirt. There were three palms, some zinnias and a yard full of dirt waiting to be landscaped. A concrete slab jutted out from the sliding door to the bedroom–white, hot, useless, unless covered with some kind of future shade construction.

Before our first child was born, we planted what we thought was a wild eucalyptus in the center of the yard. We didn't want a pool; why not a free tree? We doubted if it would grow. It looked dead. But, we left it. Spring came.

"Sam, have you noticed the little tree in the back yard? It has new leaves on it," Phyllis said.

"You're right, Honey. But these leaves don't look like Eucalyptus. I wonder what kind of tree this is? A nursery will know."

It was a rhus lancea (or African Sumac). While one of the back yard palm trees died, the rhus lancea began its long journey to the sky, spreading its branches in all directions: toward the house, reaching to the back wall, stretching to the east and west. It wasn't tall enough to give much shade yet, but it was strong enough to withstand our two daughters, Julie and Amy, as they made a playground beneath it. We should have named it. We just called it "The Tree".

I built a ramada covering the cement slab. Phyllis and the two girls planted vegetables in the planter, the zinnias having long ago gone to flower heaven.

The winter of 1969, Phyllis's parents came for a four-month stay. They camped in a small travel trailer in the back yard and Dad and I enclosed the carport, removed the storage shed and extended the first addition ten feet into the back yard. Our two-year-old son, Joe, supervised the construction after first having bacon and eggs breakfast with Grandma and Grandpa in the trailer.

The back yard had two palms, a palm frond-covered ramada, planters filled with vegetables and unwanted Bermuda grass, and "The Tree." The drive-way was white pea gravel with Bermuda grass growing through it. Our east-end yard had Bermuda grass invading our neighbor's property. Oleanders blossomed outside the patio wall. They were as tall as Tree. Our remaining palm was growing fast. Could it be that the roots had found our incoming water line?

A swing set with climbing bars provided variety for the girls play time.

The Tree grew taller, its crooked branches spreading to the roof line. I put up a two-by-four barrier to help push the limb over the roof. The patio became less of a playground and more of a gathering place for barbecues. The Tree shaded half the yard. I pruned it after a winter snow broke some of the top branches. It spread even more. There were places in the yard where the roots rose to the surface like some mysterious serpent only to submerge and resurface a short distance away. The roots headed well past the palm toward the incoming water line.

By 1980, The Tree was strong enough to handle two boys climbing. Joe and his younger brother, Rob, now made up the foursome of children using The Tree's shade and limbs for climbing and building tree houses. Our cats liked the high-up perch from which to survey their territory, or just to snooze and dream of their ancestors of the jungle. Birds visited, always keeping a wary eye out for a cat.

In summer, tents sprouted in the yard. The four children spent hours setting them up and sleeping overnight. The girls got the best, roomiest one, of course, leaving their younger brothers with the smaller one. Support ropes were strung across to The Tree for secure anchoring.

In all too short a time, the yard became quiet with only an echo of children's voices. The girls, now grown, were living elsewhere in Tucson. Joe had moved to an apartment. Rob remained to help in the yard, to prune The Tree and to finish high school.

In 1989, the ramada came down and was replaced by a 500 square-foot "Arizona Room" that extended the length of the house. Screened windows and four skylights kept this room bright all year round. The south-reaching limb of The Tree had to be cut off for the roof to extend properly. A picnic table was added. The patio planter was filled with vegetables, flowers and herbs. The Tree shaded the total area. The east palm was seventy-five feet tall and growing old. The other palm, a different variety, grew fat, spreading its fronds to meet the limbs of The Tree.

The yard man said he knew how to lay bricks and stucco walls. The man said he could fix the gates so they would swing easily. The man said he knew how to make brick planters. The man said he wouldn't hurt The Tree. A third of the patio was changed from a dirt/Bermuda mix to pleasing pastel bricks of gray and rose. A two-foot planter was built around the base of Tree adding suffocating dirt above the base line. The major "sea-serpent" root suddenly disappeared, hacked away without my knowing, and overlaid with bricks. The job was completed.

The Tree began to die. Sections of limbs turned brown and leaves began dropping. An expert was called to advise us.

"You might lose it. See here: the dirt in this planter is too high and the tree is unable to adapt. You must water this planter heavily, daily for several weeks. Let the water soak deeply. It will send out new, deep roots to compensate for the lost root. Cut back all the dead branches and control the suckers that will start growing. Prune it carefully. Wherever there are no bricks, flood the ground regularly. If you're careful, it might save itself."

The care became Rob's responsibility. We renamed it Rob's Tree. Each week he gave it six hours of water. Gradually, the leaves turned green and new growth developed. If we placed chairs and tables judiciously, we could use some of the new shade that was developing. Rob strung misters through the limbs for summer cooling. Rob's Tree thrived on the changes and attention. The patio was once again inviting. Mornings found the three of us sipping coffee and planning the next improvement on the yard. Rob would begin his morning routine wearing his old, sole-flapping boots to walk among the plants, digging and cultivating. The yard was full of shades and hues of green. Blue-green Mexican sage, pineapple salvia, mint, basil, onions, red peppers, jalapeno peppers, okra, cabbage and squash filled the planters. Hummingbirds discovered our flower food.

Evenings were spent with friends viewing stars through binoculars, relaxing with coffee, telling stories, laughing. The old, dying palm was cut down. We sliced the trunk up like so many carrots and placed the cut cylinders around the yard for small tables. The yard was an open invitation for friends to visit. With Rob's Tree in the center, the yard had become an oasis for peace and solitude.

The morning of July second, 1997, Rob died in his sleep.

There is a palm tree in our back yard, a palm tree and planters filled with overgrown sage, beans and peppers, a palm and planters and a brick patio, a table and a center piece: a pair of once sole-flapping garden boots with green and yellow-red coleus growing in them. And Rob's Tree stretches its branches, in a gentle arabesque, over the table, over two weeping parents.

* * *

JANUARY 2010   OUT OF THE VALLEY

How is it possible that so many years have passed? When Rob died, he was 23 years old. How old would he be now? In the beginning, the walls of our Valley of Grief were steep and dark– darker than the narrow inner gorge of the Grand Canyon.

Now the canyon has widened and Phyllis and I have a more expansive view of our new, changed world. We know that we may walk through other canyons, hopefully, not as dark, not as deep. We also know where our support system may be reached.

Thirteen years of membership in The Compassionate Friends

have taught us that we can move through our grief. We can now offer hope to new members fresh in their grief.

EARLY MORNING THOUGHTS

I thought about Rob at 1:30 this morning.

Does that seem surprising? We find nothing unusual, years later, to have moments of remembrance on a daily basis. Sometimes there are tears, but more often the thoughts cover me like a multi-colored quilt of warm, happy memories.

For the uninitiated, (and we hope you are never initiated into this exclusive membership!) you might think that, after thirteen years, we would be "over it."

Not a day goes by that Phyllis and I don't remember Rob. That's not to say that we are crying each day, or that we are depressed, or that we walk around zombie-like as in the first months with that blank stare: the not-too-secret "code" of recognition at our first Compassionate Friends meetings. Now the little things give us pause – a picture on the wall of Rob standing by his car, music that he played, Marvin the Martian that was tattooed on his shoulder–and we will be flooded with memories.

For me, evenings are often when I have flashes of memory. He would be thirty-six, but I see him at twenty-three, at the beginning of his maturity. I see his smile and his delightful way of bringing joy to our family and to his young niece. How he would enjoy his added nieces and nephews and they him!

Rob's Tree, the invasive rhus lancea, was removed two years ago and replaced with a desert acacia. His sole-flapping boots are buried next to the young tree.

The night is quiet. I like to think that his spirit is watching over our family. These thoughts are comforting.

That wasn't the way our grief was in the beginning.
But it is now.

Sam Turner is a native of Arizona. Sam grew up on the South Rim of Grand Canyon. He is a graduate of Pepperdine College and received his M.Ed. from the University of Arizona. He served with the Arizona Education Association Innovative Teaching Techniques Cadre as a Trainer of Trainers in Facilitating and retired from a thirty-five year teaching career (TUSD) in 1995.

He is a freelance writer having contributed to Arizona Highways *and* The Aviation *and* Business Journal, *and has taught memoir writing and beginning astronomy through Pima Community College.*

Sam and his wife, Phyllis, are co-editors of Walking this Valley, *the monthly newsletter for the Tucson Chapter of The Compassionate Friends offering guidance, comfort and hope for parents who had experienced the death of a child. Their son, Robert, died of a sleep disorder July 2, 1997 at age twenty-three. They have three surviving children.*

Sam and Phyllis have published This Might Help, A Three-Year Walk Through The Valley With The Compassionate Friends. *The book is a compilation of monthly columns published in the Tucson Chapter newsletter. Visit the website: http://members. cox.net/thismighthelp/.*

Messages from Dad
By Carol Costa

An actual séance with a person who can truly communicate with the spirits of those who have died is very different from the ones Hollywood movies portray. The first séance I attended was with a small group of women at a friend's home. Other than the woman who opened her home to us, the only other person I knew in the room was my youngest sister.

Roberta, the psychic that conducted the séance, began by telling us what to expect. "No objects will fly around the room. I will speak in the same voice I am using now. Those who have crossed over exist in another plane and I am able to communicate with them by allowing myself to tune into their frequency. Most of the spirits show me pictures and symbols that I will describe to you. It is important that you pay close attention and try to identify a spirit as your loved one. Once the connection between you and the spirit is made, it strengthens the lines of communication."

Almost immediately a spirit came in and was claimed by one of the women in the room. As the first spirit began to fade, I felt a tingling sensation on my right side but didn't say anything until Roberta said a man was present standing next to me.

"I've been thinking about my Father," I said. "Could it be him?"

Roberta smiled. "This is a man who would walk a mile to play a practical joke."

Her words captured the very essence of my Dad's personality. He was indeed a prankster who took great delight in catching people off-guard and making them laugh. He had died of lung cancer at 49. Now Roberta said he was puffing out his chest letting her know that he was free of the disease that had taken him from us.

My Father showed Roberta that he was with a religious man wearing brown robes and they were having a wonderful time in their new existence. I didn't know who that man could be and the next day I had to ask my mother about him.

"Your Dad was very close to Father Andy, the Carmelite priest who married us. They wear brown robes and Father Andy died a year or so before your Dad died. That has to be who he is with."

Other messages passed through Roberta to my sister and me that we didn't understand. One was about a young man walking a dangerous tight-rope and falling to the ground causing my Dad to be very worried about him. He showed Roberta falling leaves to indicate that this would happen in the fall. A few months later, in October of that year, we discovered that my youngest son was into drugs and had to be sent to a rehab center.

Another message I received at that first séance was about my writing career. Roberta kept saying Dad was showing her bones in the desert and that it was something important I had to write about. We guessed that it had something to do with archeology which I had no interest in whatsoever. A year later, I completed a screenplay about a psychic and my sister who had been at the séance with me read it and called me on the phone.

"I just read the scene in your script about the psychic directing the police to the place in the desert where the remains of a missing girl were found. Bones in the desert," my sister said. "This is the story that Dad said you had to write."

I had written the story, but had not connected it with the message from my Dad at the séance until my sister reminded me of it.

The other message that my dad gave us at the séance was that he was staying strong so he could help my mother when it was her time to cross over. Indeed several years later as our mother lay in a coma, my sister and I felt the presence of our Father and knew he was there in the hospital room with us. A few minutes later our Mother passed over from this life into the next to join him once again.

Carol Costa is a co-author of this book.

Two Miracles: Life and Death
By Donna Connolly

If you have ever witnessed a birth then you have truly witnessed a miracle. You have just a brief moment to feel that special miracle. I have witnessed births and deaths, and I can tell you from the bottom of my heart and soul that death is truly a special moment and as much a miracle as a baby's birth.

My mother gave me a precious spiritual gift when she passed. It was a warm Monday night in August. I sat quietly at the foot of her bed when I felt her soul go right through me. I did not know at the time what it was, but believe me, I knew it was very special. What a gift it was for me to witness her passing. It was so serene and I knew my mother was at peace.

To this day I can feel my mother around me. I smell her perfume, and once she sent me an angel. My husband, my cousin and I were on an Alaskan cruise. A terrifying storm hit the seas. Fifty-six foot thundering waves pounded the ship. Frightened, I was laying in my cabin when I saw her. She came through the closed sliding glass door. She was the most beautiful angel, the very first I have ever seen. Her face was blurred, but she glowed pure white light and I knew she was female. I knew my mother had sent her to calm our fears. Then she took her huge wings and held me close to her side, next my cousin, and then my husband. The peace that came over me that night was a miracle. I have never felt anything like it again. The angel and all three of us rode the waves together and when the storm was over she left the same way she arrived, right through the glass cabin door.

Then my Dad became ill, and if death could be beautiful then my Dad's death surely was. The family stood around his bedside and we sang songs and recited the twenty-third Psalms. I could smell and taste death, yet when the moment came, it was just a second. I felt so calm, knowing Dad was peacefully on the other side. I still feel him around me. I walk the beach daily, weather permitting, and my Dad comes along with me. I know he watches over me.

Then my dear husband of 49 years died. I met him when I was only thirteen and he was fourteen. At seventeen he joined the Army, and the same year we married. When I lost him, I knew the gift he had given me was to really and truly know and feel what a soul is. As my husband was preparing to cross over, I was guiding him to follow the light and I whispered in his right ear that I loved him very much and when he got to the other side to give me a sign that he had arrived safely. Two nights after he passed, I felt his nose on my nose and his lips touch mine. Then I smelled the mints. While alive, he always had mints in his mouth. I smiled and said, "I knew you made it." Then he was gone. I felt the most wonderful moment anyone could ever have. Now it has been almost twenty months and he still comes to me with smells of toast. He loved toast. I now know from my soul that I will be with him when I cross over.

To lose a husband, or anyone for that matter, is very hard. God has given me a very special gift. When I witness death I can feel and see a very beautiful and very peaceful moment. It is only a moment, but I can tell you without a doubt it is beautiful. I feel all my loved ones around me, and I truly believe that I will be with my husband forever and ever when I pass. Until then my life mission in to be with others to help them cross over, as it is a special moment and a very beautiful one. God Bless and So It Is.

Happiness Awaits You!

Donna Connolly has always enjoyed working with people. She has worked as a health aide, and food/ beverage server before retiring from Taj Mahal Casino in Atlantic City. She still has the desire to work with people and that is why she assists people who are ready to cross over. She loves to be still and see nature as it truly is, and watch the birds and geese from her waterfront home in N.J. She states that birds can tell us a thing or two if you have the time to watch. She also loves dancing with friends and especially her grandchildren. Donna is a lady who truly is loving life, and an inspiration for us all. She states that she is "just a lady here on earth to learn, play and love. I've had a lot of sadness in my life, but when I look back I have learned and grown I want to keep on going 'till God takes me home to be with him and my love ones. What a day of celebration that is going to be." She may be contacted by e-mail at: traveler1219@ymail. com.

Hilda
By Carol Costa

Hilda sat behind me in the alto section of our church choir. When we met she was in her eighties, but had a zest for life that many women half her age did not possess. Hilda loved music and had played the piano and sang since she was a small child.

Every other year, the choir put on a musical variety show called The Carousel. Although the choir sponsored the event, it was open to everyone in the parish who wanted to sing, dance, play a musical instrument or take part in comedy skits or excerpts from Broadway musicals. Hilda loved the shows and always took part in them. As a writer, I often wrote skits for The Carousel and directed some segments of the shows. The Carousel drew people from all over town and was a wonderful fundraiser for our church and the choir.

Hilda continued to sing and take part in the shows well into her nineties and became the oldest member of our church choir. Somewhere around her ninety-seventh birthday, Hilda's health began to fail and she was no longer able to come to practices and sing in the choir. About that time, I became a Eucharist Minister for our church and began taking weekly communion to Hilda and other people in the parish who were no longer able to attend church services.

I took communion to Hilda every Wednesday morning and always sat and visited with her for awhile. She was full of stories about her life and told me over and over again how her father had worked as a piano maker and introduced her to music at a very young age. After awhile, Hilda could no longer live alone and became a resident at a small group home. I continued to bring her communion every week and spend time talking and laughing with her. Hilda often told me she was ready to die and actually got upset when I had to tell her that someone younger than her 99 years had passed away. Finally, a few weeks before she reached her hundredth year on earth, Hilda had a stroke and died peacefully in her sleep.

Although I understood that she had been ready to move on, losing Hilda was very hard on me. I missed her and our weekly visits and grieved for months over her death. Then one Sunday afternoon, a psychic who was well known for his ability to communicate with the dead came to town and spoke at a gathering I attended. During the course of his talk, he reached out to several people in the room who had lost loved ones and gave them messages from the other side. Let me stress that I did not know this psychic and had never set eyes on him before the day of that gathering.

Suddenly, the man turned to me and said. "A very elderly woman has come into the room and has a message for you." At first, I didn't know who he could be talking about, but then he said. "She wants you to know that she is very happy and that there is wonderful music on the other side." It was then that I thought it might be Hilda. A few seconds later, the young man said, "She's showing me a carousel and says when you arrive you will put one on together."

The psychic thought the message concerned a carnival ride, but I understood immediately that Hilda was reminding me of the fun we'd had doing the church shows and telling me we would enjoy them again on the other side.

So many dear friends from our church choir have passed away, but I know that we will meet again to sing, dance, and laugh as we recreate the magic of The Carousel shows we all loved so much.

Carol Costa is a co-author of this book.

Hats of Happiness
By Michele Hirata

The summer before my Mother died, I went to stay with her for five weeks with my two-year old daughter, four-month old son and our two dogs. While my husband prepared to move our family from Virginia to California, I took the kids and the dogs to stay in Mom's two-bedroom, 700 square foot house in east Texas. It was crazy crowded, sweltering hot and my mother and I got on each other's last nerve, but I know in my heart that she knew how much I loved her.

Then, just two weeks after my family moved to California before we had even unpacked, my brother called to tell me the end was near and that Mom wanted me to fly back to Texas to be with her. I told my brother to tell Mom I wasn't coming, that I'd already told her goodbye and I wasn't strong enough to see her die. It took me four days to get on an airplane and walk into the hospital room. That was the hardest thing I've ever had to do. It was also one of the most rewarding things I've ever done in my life.

On August 27, 2003 Mom died of breast cancer. She fought this horrible disease for 17 years with radiation and chemotherapy. Her biggest challenge through the cancer was losing her hair and never feeling comfortable wearing a wig. She just couldn't be herself and I hated that for her. But I just couldn't fix it, no matter what I said or did.

The day before Mom died she was angry, not because she was dying but because she was always so afraid of everything. She was afraid of failure, afraid of what people thought of her and afraid of what she hadn't done with her life. She told me, "Michele, there's nothing to be afraid of. I see that now. Go live life, really live life. Do what you love. Promise me you'll do this." I made the promise.

In September 2003, I asked my mother-in-law to teach me to crochet to help me keep my mind off losing my mother and to keep my mother's spirit alive. She taught me how to crochet and eventually I taught myself to knit and began experimenting with hat patterns.

Six months later, at 2 a.m. on a chilly winter night, I finished my first hat crafted out of the most comfortable material I knew, a t-shirt. I designed the hat to be comfortable, fun and functional for people who had lost their hair due to illness or chemotherapy. I wanted a hat so special and fun that when hair-loss patients ventured out and about, the hat would be the conversation piece, not their disease. I spent months perfecting these little happy hats. I lost a lot of sleep but knew this was what I wanted to do. I was happy doing it.

I started donating hats to hair loss victims, hospitals, and various charities. The response was enormous and unanimous. I was overwhelmed at the impact my hats made. Everybody wanted one and the hats made people smile.

Recipients of the hats would call me, send me thank you letters and let me know how much I had changed their lives with my silly little hats. One lady said, "Michele, you have given me hope that the world really is a place of love and compassion. I cannot believe you would go through so much trouble for a complete stranger. You have turned my tears into laughter and I know after I am gone, the world will be just fine. This hat is the hope I needed." She ended her letter with, "Your mother would be so proud of you."

These words are repeated in many letters I receive. Without fail, I'm overwhelmed to tears, knowing that my mother is still here with me. I know that somehow, one way or another, she is smiling down on me and that she would be incredibly proud of what I am doing in her honor.

Michele Hirata a.k.a. Fat Thumb Chick, designs, makes and distributes Fat Thumb Chemo Beanies knitted from T-shirt material to cancer centers, hospitals and non-profit organizations worldwide, free of charge. She donates one-of-a-kind handbags and shawls to many worthwhile not-for-profit organizations to bring them much needed funding. Every Fat Thumb Michele creates is gift from her heart. Since February 2004, Michele has given away over 2,000 hats, purses and scarves to those battling a hair loss illness and worthwhile charitable organizations, worldwide. If you know someone in need of love and a smile, visit her website: www.fatthumb.com.

STEPPING STONES

Grief is a complex, individualized process. You must find your own path to restore hope and trust. Here are some ideas for your consideration:

Activity: If you have lost a loved one, seek a local bereavement support group. There is no better support than other people who share your situation.

Activity: Take stock.
What are your sources of strength?

_____

_____

_____

_____

Who or what are your sources of inspiration do you have?

_____

_____

_____

_____

On whom or what can you rely during difficult times?

_____

_____

_____

_____

What can you do to summon this support?

_____

_____

_____

_____

What role models do you have to get through difficult times?

_____

_____

_____

_____

Happiness Awaits You!

List some of the organizations in your area that counsel and support people who have suffered a loss.

_____

_____

_____

_____

CHAPTER 11

The Power of Forgiveness

Regardless of how kind we try to be, each of us have been hurt by someone else, and each of us has hurt someone else. Just as we must apologize and ask forgiveness when we do wrong, it's only fair that we forgive those who wrong us.

Sometimes that's not easy. When someone hurts us, there is a natural resistance to responding with kindness. But forgiveness is not approval for what occurred. Forgiveness is not 'letting someone off the hook'. Forgiveness is an acknowledgement that we all make mistakes.

"But you don't understand," you may protest. "They were wrong! They hurt me badly! Why should I forgive them?" Well, ask yourself this: would you rather be right or would you rather be healed? If you want to heal, you must forgive them.

Truthfully, forgiveness is letting YOU off the hook: it's a way to release the pain, the anger, the fear and the resentment we experience when someone hurts us. Forgiveness gives us the opportunity to heal and move on.

The alternatives don't work. Lashing back or seeking revenge is never as satisfying as we imagine. Harsh actions injure us in the long run. Holding grudges and hard feelings against those who have harmed us hurts us much more than it affects them.

The longer we let resentments fester, the more we are damaging our own happiness. It's impossible to be happy if we are bearing burdens from the past. Who does it serve if you are walking around bitter and seething about something that happened a decade ago, while the person who hurt you can't even remember your name, let alone the incident? Grudges hurt you, not them.

"But it's too late," you may say. No, it isn't. When you hurt someone, it's better to apologize immediately, of course. But it's better to apologize late than not at all. Forgiveness works the same way. We can be way overdue when it comes to forgiving others. But as soon as we do, we can heal. And we can't move forward until we forgive.

"But I don't even know where they are, what they're doing, if they are even alive," you might counter. It doesn't matter. If you can forgive someone in person, it's powerful. But you can also forgive someone without them knowing anything about it. It doesn't matter where they are or what they're doing. You have the power to forgive them, right here, right now.

Forgiveness is really a gift you give yourself. You'll feel the difference in your own heart when you truly forgive someone. There's a little shift, deep down. It feels like relief. It's the first step to replacing the pain of the incident with peace and joy.

Now, its one thing to forgive someone else, it's another to forgive yourself. Many of us are hard on ourselves. We punish ourselves for mistakes we've made. But if we insist on carrying negative experiences from our past, we are needlessly denying ourselves happiness in the present.

We need to forgive ourselves. We deserve being treated kindly and compassionately – even by ourselves. As human beings, we all make mistakes. Whatever it is, forgive yourself. You deserve the same courtesy you would give someone else. Imagine the relief of truly forgiving yourself. Picture yourself laying those unnecessary burdens down and stepping into happiness.

That is the power of forgiveness.

I Am a Happy Man
By Bill Pelke

I am a happy man. I am happy because I know I am making a difference in the world.

Recently a representative of the popular TV show, Women on Death Row, contacted me. She said they were in their fifth season of production and that they were going to do a story about the Paula Cooper case.

Paula Cooper is the girl who was sentenced to death for killing Nana, my grandmother.

The representative told me that their series included interviews with victims' families and their feelings about the situation. She told me that in researching the Paula Cooper case they had read something about me. She told me they rarely came up with a victims' family member like me. I smiled when she said that. I knew what she meant.

I told her about the night my feelings about Paula Cooper changed. It was on November 2, 1986, the turning point of my life. That night in the crane was my "mountaintop" experience.

First I need to tell you about Nana. To the world she was known as Ruth Elizabeth Pelke, Bible Teacher. Her grandchildren, who loved her dearly, called her Nana. She was a very religious woman and was a true servant of God. Her passion was telling young children Bible stories by the old fashioned means of "the flannel graph board." I learned Bible stories as a child watching Nana tell of Noah and the Ark, Daniel in the Lion's Den, Joseph and his Coat of Many Colors (my favorite) and many others. When I married and had children, I watched again as Nana told my kids and their friends these wonderful Bible stories. It is what she loved to do.

When three ninth grade students knocked on Nana's door on May 14, 1985, she invited them into her home. They told her they wanted to take Bible lessons from her. Even though the girls were a little older than most of the kids Nana taught, it was

233

one more chance for her to share her faith with young people and she let them into her home.

Nana was brutally stabbed to death on the dining room floor of her home. Paula Cooper was sentenced to death for her role in the robbery-murder.

Fast forward to November 2, 1986. I was at work, sitting high above the ground in the cab of my overhead crane. I began to think about Nana and her Christian faith. I began to think about three things that Jesus had to say about forgiveness. He told the multitudes to forgive if they wanted their Heavenly Father to forgive them. He told Peter that seven times was not enough when it came to forgiveness. He said seventy times seven.

In the Bible, the number seven is a symbol of perfection. I knew he didn't mean to forgive four hundred and ninety times and then we don't have to forgive any more. He was telling Peter that when you forgive that many times it would become a habit. Forgive, forgive and keep on forgiving. I also envisioned Jesus on the cross and pictured the crown of thorns on his brow and the nails in his hands and feet. I recalled Jesus saying, "Father forgive them for they know not what they are doing." I realized Paula Cooper did not know what she was doing.

I thought that anyone in their right mind, anyone who knew what they were doing, would not take a 12 inch butcher knife and stab someone 33 times. I knew that it was a crazy, crazy, senseless act. I knew I was being called by my faith to forgive. I concluded that I should forgive. Maybe someday I would.

I recalled the day that Paula Cooper was sentenced to death. As the judge began to deliver the sentence of death, an old man in the galley, sitting a few rows in front of me began wailing, "They are going to kill my baby. They are going to kill my baby." The judge ordered the bailiff to escort the man from the courtroom because he was disrupting the proceedings. I watched as the old man was led past me and saw the tears streaming down his cheeks. He was Paula Cooper's grandfather.

I knew that Nana would not have wanted this old man to have to go through the experience of seeing a granddaughter that he loved very much, strapped in the electric chair and have volts of electricity put to her until she was dead. I knew she would not wish this on that old man.

I thought about Paula Cooper. I recalled as they led her off to death row, her tears were falling making big splotches on her blue prison dress. I had supported the judge's sentence of death but I knew it would not bring Nana back.

I began to think how Nana had let Paula into her house because she wanted to share her faith and love of God with her. I felt that Nana would have wanted someone to try to give that message to Paula.

As I envisioned the image of Nana, tears were in her eyes and streaming down her cheeks. I knew that they were tears of love and compassion for Paula Cooper and her family. I felt Nana wanted someone in my family to have the same sort of love and compassion as she did. I felt like it fell on my shoulders.

I said a short prayer. I begged God to give me love and compassion for Paula Cooper and her family, and to please do so on behalf of Nana. Suddenly, a thought occurred to me: I could write Paula Cooper a letter. I could tell her the kind of person Nana was and share some Bible passages that I thought Nana would like me to share. I also realized that I wanted to help her in any way that I could, that I no longer wanted her to die. I wanted to get her death sentence overturned. My prayer of compassion had been answered.

I learned the most important lesson of my life that night. It was about the healing power of forgiveness. When my heart was touched with compassion, forgiveness happened automatically. I realized that the killing of another person would not bring healing. It was at that moment of forgiveness that real healing began. I believe this kind of healing is what the families of all murder victims need.

As I sat up in my crane cab that night, I felt so profoundly different; I knew my life had changed significantly. I knew God had touched my heart and He did so for a reason. I made God two promises that night. First, that any success that came into my life as a result of forgiving Paula Cooper, I would give God the honor and glory for it, because it was God who had touched my heart. It was nothing I had done.

The second promise I made was that I would walk through any door that opened as a result of forgiving Paula Cooper. If I had known that night what doors would open, I would have been too scared to make that promise. I can say to this day I have kept both of those promises I made that night.

I got involved in an international campaign that led to Paula Cooper being taken off of death row. I talked about forgiveness on programs like Oprah, Good Morning America, Geraldo, PM Magazine and Sally Jesse Raphael. Magazines such as *Parade, Woman's Day, Ebony, Sassy, Psychiatry Today* and numerous newspapers gave me the opportunity to share my story.

In 1991 I participated in a march that went from death row in Florida to Atlanta, Georgia. Sister Helen Prejean, who later authored *Dead Man Walking*, led the march. On that march I dedicated my life to the abolition of the death penalty. I vowed anytime a state or country killed one of its own citizens, I would stand up and say it was wrong.

I helped Murder Victims Families for Reconciliation (MVFHR) incorporate into a non-profit so that the voices of other murder victims' families could be heard in the death penalty abolition movement.

I never could have imagined the doors that have opened since that night. Going through those doors has brought me continued happiness. Why? Because I know I have made, and am still making a difference in this world. Each of the above mentioned organizations are helping move toward worldwide abolition of the death penalty. It is definitely a joy to know I am making a difference while working for a cause I believe in. Making the world a better place is all that I can hope for. It is wonderful to watch it happen.

People told me I was crazy to forgive Paula, much less try to get her death sentenced overturned. My response always was that forgiving Paula did more for me than it did for her. That is how forgiveness works. Forgiveness frees you up to do more than you ever thought possible, because you get rid of the heavy weight around your neck that drags you down.

When I was on the Oprah Winfrey show years ago, she pointed out that forgiveness was the major tenant of all the major religions. I have tried to live a life of forgiveness since my night in the crane. It is a wonderful way to live.

I know that the answer is not revenge. Revenge is never, ever the answer. The answer is love and compassion for all of humanity. Compassion will bring you the healing power of forgiveness. And that will bring you happiness.

Bill Pelke is the President and cofounder of Journey of Hope... from Violence to Healing *and has authored a book with the same name. Having dedicated his life to the abolition of the death penalty, Bill is on the board of the National Coalition to Abolish the Death Penalty, Murder Victims Families for Human Rights and Alaskans Against the Death Penalty. He is a founding member of the World Coalition to Abolish the Death Penalty and Murder Victims Families for Reconciliation. Bill is also a cofounder of the Abolitionist Action Committee and the Annual Fast and Vigil at the US Supreme Court. Visit his website: www. journeyofhope.org*

The Question That Changed My Life
By Kitty Chappell

I was nineteen years old when I was asked to grant an unfathomable forgiveness. Following church one Sunday, an older woman stopped me to chat. Abruptly she asked, "Have you forgiven your father?"

My father was in jail post trial, waiting transport to the state prison for the premeditated attempted murder of my mother. Mom's head wounds had not even healed. How dare she even suggest forgiveness! I mumbled something about how I didn't think I'd have to worry since my father would never ask my forgiveness for anything.

"You're probably right, but you still need to forgive him."

"Why should I do that? I've lived in fear all of my life for my mother and younger siblings. Dad bragged how he'd kill us, claim temporary insanity, and get away with it if we attempted to escape. And that's just what he tried to do. Thank God, mother survived. And he was sentenced to only three and a half years for premeditated attempted murder! Is that justice? No, I won't forgive him!"

"I understand, but you still need to forgive him."

"I'd like to know just who would expect me to do that!"

She replied softly, "God."

I glared at her, and then ran down the steps.

Our house sold quickly and our hurting family moved from Texas to beautiful Southern California. This is the new beginning I need, I thought, now I can be happy. But I wasn't happy. I felt moody, depressed, and angry. The woman's question popped into my mind. "Have you forgiven your father?" I tried to ignore it, but it seemed that every time I opened the Bible, the scriptures referred to forgiveness. "Forgive, if you have anything against anyone." And again: "Father, forgive them," Jesus pled from the cross.

Even the books I read chided me. "Forgiveness is not an emotion," Corrie ten Boom wrote as a survivor of a World War II concentration camp, "it is an act of the will." She explained she couldn't forgive through her own strength, but with God's help she did.

Finally I admitted one day, "Lord, I'd like to be able to forgive my father, because this resentment is eating me up inside, but I have a problem—I don't want to. Can you help me to want to forgive my father?" This became my daily prayer.

Some months later, I was overwhelmed with a sudden desire to forgive my father. I really wanted to. I whispered, "I forgive you, Dad, for everything!" My tears flowed freely, washing away all of my resentment.

Yet little did I know that when I forgave my father that day, it opened my heart to an ongoing power, a power that would enable me to forgive him one final time, at another tragic time and place.

For many years we lived in fear that my father would find us after his release from prison and carry out his threats to "get us" since he blamed us for his conviction. But we never heard from him, not until almost thirty years later.

Our father located and contacted us three children, and asked our forgiveness. He was in poor health and appeared remorseful for his wasted years. We learned that following prison, he had re-married and had a grown, married son. We reluctantly allowed him into our lives, believing he was just a sickly old man, longing to have some contact before he died with the children he had once abused. After some time, we cautiously visited him and his wife, Mary, in another city, and they later visited me and my family in our home.

Mary and I became friends, but I soon learned Dad had told her only what he wanted her to know about his past—that his first wife was "bad" and he'd beaten her too severely because of it, but it was because he was "sick"—and he'd spent a short time in prison.

We never told Mary the truth because she was a loving, kind individual and we saw no reason to hurt her or her son. They couldn't help what my Dad did in his past, just as we couldn't. Mary said she didn't understand why we had ignored our father all those years. Oh how I was tempted to tell her, but my only response was "Dad wasn't the best of fathers to us but our mother was a very good mother."

Mary responded "You father may be controlling, but he has never physically abused us."

However, some months later we received a phone call and learned that Dad had driven their car over a cliff in a murder/ suicide attempt. Mary was thrown clear but Dad suffered internal injuries. At the accident scene, Mary told the police of Dad's deliberate actions, how he drove over the cliff despite her screams of "Please don't do this!" Dad was hospitalized and put under house arrest.

After release from the hospital, my father was sent to jail pending his hearing. Mary called me often. She said Dad had an incurable disease and had become obsessed with death. He feared he would die and didn't want to leave his younger wife and his property for some other man to enjoy. Her voice broke as she admitted that he had started accusing her of having an affair.

My throat tightened and my heart pounded with realization. It was then that I told Mary the truth about Dad's past, leaving nothing out.

"Mary, you've got to leave! Dad accused my mom of the same thing before he tried to murder her. He lied in court saying she and I were prostitutes and that's why he lost control. He had always told us to never tell anyone of his abuse or try to escape because if we did he would kill us all and plead temporary insanity. However, with the help of relatives we did leave, but he found us. That's why he tried to murder Mom, as a punishment. He lied about Mom and me to establish grounds for his temporary insanity plea."

"But he has never hit me," Mary responded. "There were many times when he looked like he was going to, but he didn't."

"That's because of his prison record. The thought of returning to jail terrified him. You told me yourself that he swore he would never go to prison again, and he won't."

I finally convinced Mary that she should tell the judge not to release Dad pending his hearing because her life would be in danger. But Dad's attorney convinced the judge that it was an accident and that Mary had been given bad information by a vindictive daughter from a previous bad marriage. Despite Mary's pleas, the judge released my father to his own recognizance and ordered him to appear in six weeks for his hearing.

When Mary called me with this news I was terrified for her. "You've got to leave, now! Dad will kill you. I know how he thinks, Mary. He has a terminal condition from which there is no escape and he faces the possibility of prison. He believes you betrayed him by telling the officers at the accident scene what really happened. He will punish you. Only this time he'll not use a car, he'll use a gun."

"There's no place for me to go," she said sadly. "I'd be afraid to go to my parent's house. "That's the first place he'd look."

"Go anywhere, Mary; just get away while you can!"

With a false note of hope in her voice, she said "I really think I'll be okay. Thank you for everything, Kitty. I have to go now and pick him up."

"Please call me when you get a chance," I begged. "I need to know what's happening."

"If I can, I will," she promised.

Hot tears trickled down my face. "I'll pray for you, and for Dad that he will listen to God's voice and not do what I'm afraid he will do."

That was the last time we spoke.

Six weeks later, when Dad did not appear for his hearing, two deputy sheriffs were dispatched to Dad's home to arrest him. There they found the bodies of Dad and Mary, dead from gunshot wounds.

I sat motionless at the double funeral. My heart was heavy and tempted to ask, "Why, God?" But it remained quiet. It knew the answer. Dad had made many wrong choices throughout his life, and, tragically, this was his final wrong choice.

As I sat there I suddenly realized that had I not already forgiven my father for his past wrongs, this current tragedy would simply revive burning embers of hate. I would relive in vivid detail all of the horrors of my father's past violence, particularly his gruesome near fatal attack on my mother as she lay sleeping. I would become even more enraged, with yet another layer of anger wound bitterly around my soul. I would have sat there out of stoic loyalty to Mary, hating my father, glaring grim-faced and tight-lipped at the two caskets. I would have shaken my fists mentally toward heaven, demanding an answer to "Why, God?"

Instead, I sat in the midst of a double tragedy, not as a bedraggled, hate-filled survivor, but as a victorious overcomer overwhelmed with God's sweet peace. I grieved over the tragic loss of Mary, but rejoiced in the knowledge that she was in heaven.

I felt compassion for my father, and a bone-chilling sadness because of his final wrong choice. Yet, my heart rejoiced because it was free!

My life had been changed forever when I forgave my father—all because of one lady's question.

Kitty Chappell's bio follows her story in Chapter 8.

Permission to Smile
By Sabine Huemer

As a university student in my home country of Austria, I spent a good portion of every summer in Switzerland as a Serviertochter (literally translated as "service daughter"), the Swiss name for a temporary waitress with little or no service experience. High-end Swiss resort hotels, dependent on seasonal tourism, pay high hourly wages but avoid even more costly benefits as they fill these jobs with overqualified and undertrained young women from neighboring countries.

The beginning of every July, my girlfriends and I packed our black skirts and white blouses and took the train through the Austrian Alps into Switzerland. One summer the destination was Zermatt, at the foothill of the Matterhorn, another was Saas-Fee, surrounded by the highest peaks of the Swiss Alps. No matter where we went, we were greeted by spectacular scenery, dizzying mountain air, and an earful of Schwyzerduetsch, the Swiss German that is mostly unintelligible to anyone but the Swiss.

Ready to report for duty, we were spread across the property to service the exclusive international clientele in the guest dining hall, the elegant restaurant, the casual bistro, or the golf club house. Our first day of work marked the beginning of eight weeks of intense physical labor that let us forget all about who we were back home, the books we had read, the classes we had taken, the ambitions we had harbored. We were now waitresses and our job demanded us to be well-organized, quick on our feet, friendly but demure with an awareness of basic dining etiquette: know how to set a table, don't take away plates before everyone is done, serve from the right.

The breath-taking Alpine setting became a backdrop that we only noticed again on our day of departure. Our days were now filled with work and our evenings with stories about our mishaps and embarrassments of the day: noodle soup quietly spilled into the German fashion designer's open purse, a steak served to the Swiss millionaire golfer sliding off the plate into his lap, a Campari Soda splashing over the dress of the Saudi-Arabian prince's girlfriend who had asked for "a splash" of Seltzer. Some of us fell in love with a cook or a guest but neither the flings nor the stories told lasted longer than the day we went back on that train and resumed our ordinary lives.

There were many stories left untold during those nightly gatherings on our bunk beds: occurrences with no punch line, no entertainment value, stories that didn't help relieve the stress built up during the work day. Service personnel and cooks have been known to run through dining halls threatening guests with kitchen knives or jumping out dorm windows naked when the pressure became too much. We had our stories to keep us sane. And our stories were disposable. After they had served their purpose we tossed them from our minds. They never became memories.

So, it is not a story after all that I will tell but a simple human interaction that has stuck with me for over two decades. It is a memory I recall when needed. It may start with a slight, an insult, an inconsiderate gesture, perhaps by a loved one, maybe a total stranger, that turns into an unpleasant memory that does not go away easily. I will sense a certain nagging in my mind, a feeling of disappointment and hurt that can quickly grow into anger if not dealt with swiftly. The only way to truly shake off that unpleasant feeling is through forgiveness, a conccpt so elusive and broad that most of us never manage to master it. Still, deep down we know that the only way we can make room for happiness again is to clear our mind from this nuisance. Here is what I learned back then in the Swiss Alps:

On one of my tours, I started out working in the guest dining room with a tight-knit crew of professional Italian waiters who shielded me like a little sister from any unpleasant experiences. But due to a shortness of staff in the rustic restaurant, which served local specialties to hotel guests and locals alike, I was transferred and relentlessly exposed to the tough local crowd; businessmen who placed their orders in the heaviest Schwyzerduetsch to test how much the new Austrian Serviertochter was able to adapt; families who managed to order and consume a full dinner without ever making eye contact. This was their silent way of protesting the wave of foreign workers flooding their land every summer and winter. Each day I held my breath for foreigners to occupy my serving station.

It was the omen to one of those dreadful evenings, when an elderly, gnomish-looking local couple sat down at one of my tables. My heart sank a little when I saw their grim faces. Prepared for another challenge from hard-headed mountain folks, I went over and took their order amidst a packed restaurant, then relayed it to a busy kitchen, filled with steam and adrenaline. The smooth start of our interaction came to an abrupt halt when I served the plates and the little man hissed at me angry-faced that I had delivered the wrong dish for his wife. I silently cursed his twisted dialect, the root cause of our issue, as he threw a few unnecessary insults at me, and then left to tend to my more pleasant guests.

When I returned to the couple to serve her correct dish, the husband complained that his food was now cold. I was left with more wrath from the already red-hot-angry chef to get the order reheated. There was no fun in this story. No punch line. The two gnomes left after only a few bites leaving me with a few more cold glares and no tip. I wished for them to never leave the forest again.

A few busy days later, I noticed an elderly couple enter the restaurant. They seemed familiar, so I acknowledged them with a friendly wave. They did not react. On my way to drop off a bill, I swung by the entrance door and greeted them with a "Great to see you back!" They looked puzzled. Finally, as I shook their hands with a genuine, warm smile, I realized who they were, the sour forest gnomes from the other night! A hot flash ran down my spine. My smile froze, my gaze dropped. But then, something miraculous happened. When I looked up at them again, I saw two very different people in front of me: Who was this adorable older couple, faces lit up with broad smiles?

They chuckled, "Nice to see you again! Where is your station?" Still speechless, I pointed to my tables. They excitedly scurried over and sat down. That night, we truly enjoyed each other's company.

Over two decades later, I don't remember their faces, what they had ordered, or what we had talked about that night. But I remember the power and magic of forgiveness, even, or perhaps because. it came by accident. My lapse of memory gave the couple permission to smile, to forget, and forgive. And in return, I was given a moment of red-cheeked, giddy happiness. Forgiveness comes from a place of no expectation, a mind set free from memories, a purposeful case of amnesia. We all have the power to drop our pride, set our ego aside and simply hit the reset button to allow ourselves and others room for mutual enjoyment and happiness ever after.

Sabine Huemer now lives in the Los Angeles area with her husband and soon-to-be-born son. She has a Masters Degree in Psychology and conducts autism research at the University of California, Irvine, where she is currently working on a PhD in Cognitive Sciences.

Smile on Your Brother
By Maggie TerryViale

This morning I picked up a book on Reiki at my friends house. I randomly opened to a page where the words "Emanate love." were highlighted. I read the preceding paragraph on anger and how it was better to act versus react when one felt angry. Good advice I said to my friend. This is exactly what we had talked about the day before.

The phone rang, breaking the moment. A friend called to say a former roommate had posted something on her Facebook blog about me. She repeated what it said. My 'love' went out the window, and in flew rage. Whether what she was writing was truth, or not, didn't seem to matter. What mattered then was that it upset me. My peace was gone and any form of tarnished halo I might have thought I had surely crashed to my feet in a very loud thud.

I thought back to the words, act, not react, and knew they were truth. I tried to let it go, and for a while I did.

But later the anger returned with a vengeance. Hey, I'm just being honest here, what can I say. So what do we do when someone spreads gossip, cuts us off in traffic, treats us unfairly, or a mire of other things petty and small. And what of the bigger things that life presents to us, too?

Yes, we've read the books, heard of a thousand ways to cope. Breathe, let it go, walk on the beach, do yoga, meditate, write a letter and tear it up, pound a pillow or stomp the floor, breathe some more, forgive, see it as a Blessing in Disguise, accept and move on. We're all unique. What works for me may not work for you. Over the years I've learned what works best for me. I ran a hot bath and climbed in (although my blood might have been boiling enough to melt ice) I leaned my head back into the clearing water and began to breathe as deeply as I could. What to do here? My mind chattered on. I decided to give it all up to God (or substitute any Creator name that works for

247

you) I literally felt the anger spiral counter-clock wise with in me, release, and float upward with the intention that the energy would be transmuted into a more positive emotion.

I knew this person felt hurt. I knew this person had reacted without thinking. I knew this person was a child of God. I knew I needed to write this article and share this experience with you. I am now in the place to thank her. I am now in the place to breathe more deeply and act with Love. I am now in a better place to Emanate Love.

A song of old rang through my mind, those of an older generation, and maybe the current generation of beautiful, young Light Beings, too, might remember these words of wisdom:

Come on you people now
Smile on your brother
Everybody get together
Try to love one another right now

Maggie TerryViale is a co-author of this book.

Peanut Butter & Forgiveness
By Carolyn Solares

I had a huge, friendship-ending fight on a cross-country road trip with my best friend. We had been driving for ten hours in the middle of no-where. I was hungry and exhausted, always a disastrous combination for anyone around me. Accordingly, I became irrational, accusatory, and mean, falling into the same old patterns and bad habits I lugged with me into all my relationships. This tantrum was especially ironic, as we had just completed a five-day retreat. So much for my emotional and spiritual growth! I was in crisis, once again spiraling into a full-blown neurotic meltdown.

My friend was understandably distraught and incredibly angry with me. She was so mad she wanted to drive two-thousand miles home that same night. Somehow, I managed to reason with her that she had every right to be furious and hurt, but it wasn't a great idea to drive feeling that way through the mountains in the dark. So, we skipped dinner, found the only hotel with two rooms available, and escaped from each other for the night.

After taking my luggage to my room, I returned to the car to scrounge for some food. I was starving and distressed. That I had sabotaged this friendship horrified me. I pulled out a jar of peanut butter and a loaf of bread, and set them aside as I grabbed a knife and a bag carrying my toothbrush. When I reached for the peanut butter, I couldn't find it anywhere. I searched and searched. Hadn't I just had my hand on it? Had I imagined I had found it? After ten minutes of stressful searching, I decided to go back to my hotel room before I became unglued. Feeling desperate, I resigned myself to eating some plain white bread and the smashed granola bar I had found on the car floor.

Returning to my room, I rummaged through all of my bags, but could not find the peanut butter. What did turn up, however, were two tubes of toothpaste. With a groan, I realized that my friend didn't have any. Feeling sheepish, I left my room, knocked on her door, and left the toothpaste without waiting for an answer.

When I went back to my room, I discovered my door had locked behind me and I didn't have a key, just one more reminder that I had completely screwed up.

I loped downstairs to the front desk and asked for another key. Instead of going back upstairs to my room, I walked out the front door of the hotel. Without much thought, I decided to circle around the dark parking lot in one last search for the peanut butter.

Feeling as small and alone as I had ever felt, I suddenly thought to ask for help. I surprised myself by saying a prayer, which was not something I typically did, especially when I had been a complete jerk.

My prayer went something like: "God, I know I was a jerk and that I was totally wrong. I understand that and I feel truly terrible about it. But I'm getting pretty desperate here and I could really use the peanut butter." I walked a few more feet, and then stopped in my tracks. In the middle of the hotel parking lot lay the jar of peanut butter.

At first, I couldn't believe what I was seeing; I was stunned. As I picked up the jar, I shook my head and said, "No way!" then a baffled, "Thank You." The jar of peanut butter had rolled at least twenty feet from the car. Had I not given my friend the toothpaste, locked myself out of my room, and exited a different door of the hotel, I would never have found it. There was no way I could ignore this much synchronicity.

That night, I ate a lonely peanut butter sandwich in my room, wrote my friend a heartfelt note of apology, slipped the note under her door, and went to bed. In the morning, I woke up feeling better, but still sad and resigned. My friend was justifiably hurt and furious. I knew I deserved whatever was coming to me; I'd just have to take my licks. Then I had a radical thought. What if I didn't deserve to be punished? What if I deserved to be forgiven?

At that moment, something significant shifted in me and around me. After finding the peanut butter the night before, I was not opposed to asking for a little Divine help. So, I asked God to forgive me for having hurt my friend, understanding at last that I deserved forgiveness. Thirty seconds later, my friend knocked on my door. I didn't have to say anything; she had already forgiven me. We packed up our things and continued West on our cross-country boondoggle.

In the days that followed the Peanut Butter Miracle, I began to see how I had withheld forgiveness because I never felt I deserved it myself. Since I didn't deem myself worthy of forgiveness, and often thought I deserved to be punished, I couldn't see that anyone else deserved to be forgiven. I didn't discriminate in applying this rule; I was an equal opportunity grudge-holder. Like a sack of rocks, I dragged my projection and inability to forgive into all of my relationships.

What I withheld from other people, I also withheld from myself. Not forgiving myself, or anyone else, prevented me from seeing the love that other people had for me. It blocked me from seeing the love I had too. And I have to admit that sack of rocks had become really heavy.

True forgiveness requires us to open our hearts and let go of the past. For a long time, I had absolutely no idea how to open my heart this way. Thankfully, a lowly jar of peanut butter finally cut through my defenses and pride. When I most needed to be forgiven was not when I was feeling great. I needed it most when I was feeling low, alone, and ashamed.

Sure, my prayers and mental dialogue are still often along the lines of: "I am willing to be willing to forgive this person." I also have to remember that includes me. To my amazement, even these reluctant pleas provide enough of an opening. While I have swallowed a fair amount of pride learning how to forgive, it doesn't suck nearly as much as I had feared. My own experiences in being forgiven remind me that when we offer forgiveness without judgment or strings attached, we lighten the loads of everyone.

My younger brother and I hadn't spoken for over a year. Family drama, dysfunction, and reluctance to swallow our pride contributed to this estrangement. But in the month following my profound lessons in forgiveness, I began to see that the resentment and anger I held towards him weren't good for me. They couldn't possibly be good for him either. I was clinging to adolescent hostility and suffocating on my anger. How could he not feel that? I decided that if I was serious about learning to forgive, then I had better find a way to open my heart to him. Love, even at a distance, had to be better than the garbage I was spewing.

When I would feel angry and resentful, I tried to replace it with compassion. If I happened to see my brother or my sister-in-law, I tried to be decent. And I asked God to help me open my heart.

A few months after making this commitment, my brother threw a surprise birthday party for his wife. I attended the party, not because I had to, but because it was another chance to be kind. I couldn't underestimate the importance of a simple fact: my brother had invited me.

When I grabbed my jacket at the end of the evening, my brother called me over and asked if I was leaving. Then he walked outside with me, put his arm around my shoulder, and thanked me for coming. As I walked away, he said, "Love ya." Until then, I hadn't realized how much I had needed to hear that. It turns out that extraordinary things happen if I open my heart. And when I am decent and forgiving and kind, people seem to know what I need.

Carolyn Solares began her quest for happiness after realizing her once perfect-seeming life resembled a Lifetime movie. Through heartbreak and disappointment, she discovered that despite an MBA, a career, and accomplishments, she needed a much stronger foundation. After rebuilding her life, Carolyn began to write about her own journey of faith, healing, and happiness. Medical intuitive, Christel Nani, says that Carolyn's writing "embodies the energy of true healing." Carolyn's now diverse and happy life includes writing, creative consulting, design, photography, travel, and fun. Look for her book, Peanut Butter & Forgiveness, *in 2010 and visit her website: www. mundane2insane.com.*

STEPPING STONES

You've been wronged. Someone did a bad thing. Now what are you going to do about it?

1. You can stew -- keep it all inside, festering. That only hurts yourself.

2. You can play the victim. You tell everyone what a horrible thing happened to you – spread the word about what a terrible person the perpetrator of the incident is. This only prolongs negativity and spreads the pain. You can lash back -- seek revenge or payback. This may give you momentary satisfaction but it won't feel nearly as satisfying as you anticipated, and it will not heal your pain.

3. You can forgive them and move on. If you want to heal, if you want to be happy, forgiveness is the answer.

Activity: Take a moment to make a forgiveness inventory. Who do you need to forgive? What grudges are you holding?

_____

_____

_____

_____

What is it costing you to hold these resentments? How does it make you feel? How does it affect how you are living your life?

_____

_____

_____

_____

Pick someone from your initial answer, above. What benefits might there be to forgiving them? How would you feel? How might it improve your life?

_____

_____

_____

_____

Activity: Imagine this person as a child, helpless and alone. Could you have compassion for them in that circumstance? Can you acknowledge that they are a fallible human being, susceptible to making mistakes? You don't need to justify or approve of what they did. But can you forgive them?

Activity: Try this version of Ho'oponopono -- a technique derived from Hawaiian spiritual practices. Think of the person you'd like to forgive. In your heart, accept responsibility for whatever you have done that brought forth their hurtful behavior. Apologize to their spirit. Ask their forgiveness for whatever it was that caused them to act hurtfully. Ask for harmony to be restored.

Activity: Take a moment. Acknowledge that you are a fallible human, that you make mistakes and that you deserve forgiveness from them. View yourself with compassion and kindness. Forgive yourself.

CHAPTER 12

The Circle of Life

A ring is round and has no end. It is the symbol for eternity. In many cultures the hole in the center of the ring is also believed to be a gateway leading to things and events both known and unknown. Like the ring the circle of life continues forever.

While our earthly shells succumb to age and illness our inner spirits grow stronger and wiser preparing for the body's life span to end.

Whatever else you accept as true, there is no denying that no one remains on earth forever. Everyone dies and most people believe that when their souls leave their bodies they will continue to exist in another time and place. Heaven, hell, and in some religions, a place called purgatory, are presented as options for where the soul will travel after death. Are these tangible places? Are these just concepts perpetuated by religious leaders to keep you grounded in goodness? What really happens to the soul when it leaves the body? In this chapter, you will read stories written by people who have died and then returned to their bodies. They have all had what is known as a near-death experience.

Some people who have had a near-death experience claim to have entered a tunnel and traveled towards a light. Others say they viewed their bodies from a distance and had conversations with deceased relatives and friends. Still others believe that God spoke to them. All of course were sent back to their bodies to continue their lives here on earth. Most say they didn't want to come back to their bodies, which in itself is a wonderful recommendation for what awaits us when we cross the threshold that exists between life and death.

Further evidence that the soul continues after being released from the body is the ability we have of communicating with those who have crossed over. The circle of life is never ending and the happiness you attain on earth remains with you for eternity.

My Bargain with God
By Joyce Martin

I had been in and out of a comatose state since the accident. My injuries were extensive. The fact that I had been pulled from the burning car and not miscarried because of the accident was a miracle, but only the beginning in a series of unbelievable events.

From the beginning, the doctors told my family I was going to die, and if by some chance I did recover, I would never walk again or lead any semblance of a normal life. Crushed bones, internal bleeding and a multitude of other injuries had kept me unconscious most of the time. When I did fight my way back to reality for brief moments, the pain was so excruciating I could do nothing but cry out and will myself back into the blackness where I hovered between life and death.

Then late one night, my condition worsened. The attending physician explained things to my mother. "We're going to try and operate. It's her only chance, but it's a very slim one," he said gently.

"What about the baby she's carrying?" Mama asked.

The young doctor shook his head sadly, "Just another strike against her."

The trip to the operating room jostled me into a semi-conscious state. The pain was unbearable and I began to moan, then another wall of darkness seemed to descend on my body pushing it down into oblivion. As I gave myself up to the darkness once more, I heard someone call out. "We're losing her."

Then, I felt myself slipping away, off the hospital gurney. I found myself in front of a flight of stairs. I looked up and saw that they seemed to go on forever, with the top of them disappearing into a circle of dazzling bright clouds. Instinctively, I knew that if I passed through those clouds, I would be safe and warm forever.

I began to climb the stairs. At first the steps were dirty and worn, covered with debris. The pain was so severe I had to crawl, literally dragging myself across the steps. I had only one thought and that was to reach the glorious circle of light that beckoned me from above.

As I continued my trek, I realized it was becoming easier. The pain was lessening, and at the same time, the condition of the stairs was changing. Each step was nicer than the last, until they were glowing like stars, full of luminous color.

The pain disappeared completely and I ran up the beautiful iridescent staircase. Strains of music, lovely beyond description, seemed to surround me. I neared the circle of clouds with easy confident strides with no thoughts of the life I had left behind. I was only aware of this blissful sanctuary of music and light. I ran up the last few stairs, anxious to reach the dazzling clouds and be absorbed into the light.

I reached the top step and attempted to move into the clouds. Surprised and disappointed, I found myself back on the last step again. A few more unsuccessful tries puzzled me, then it was explained to me. "You must go back. Your time has not yet come. You have work to do."

I could not tell where this information was coming from, as it was not a voice with a person attached to it. It was more like a message being transmitted to me from somewhere beyond the beautiful clouds.

I really didn't care who was communicating this directive, my answer was quick and firm. "No, I'm not going back. I want to stay here."

The reply came back just as swiftly. "You must return. You have work to do. You must help others."

I didn't ask how I was supposed to help others. I didn't care. My only desire, my only thought was to stay there, so I sat down on the step determined not to leave. I was suspended between life and eternity, but then the mystical voice imparted another message. It reminded me of my children and everything I had ever wanted in life, and promised to grant me true happiness on earth if I would return and help others.

As they say, it was an offer I couldn't refuse. I accepted the bargain and began to descend the stairs, not daring to look back at the incredible beauty and peace I was leaving behind.

My journey down was a reverse of my ascension. The lovely iridescent stairs dissolved into worn out steps scattered with debris, and the pain was there too, hovering on each stair and growing stronger with each downward movement. By the time I got to the bottom I was moaning in agony. I stepped into blackness, and found myself back on the gurney.

My face was covered with a sheet. My groans soon brought someone over to investigate. The sheet was pulled back and a man looked down at me with an astonished expression. "Welcome back, honey. I thought we'd lost you," he said kindly.

Tears of pain and frustration rolled down my face, as the doctor voided my death certificate and summoned the staff to remove the morgue tag from my toe, and take me back to my room for an examination.

The examination determined that my condition was greatly improved, and my unborn child's heart was beating normally. In a flurry of activity, I was hooked back up to IV's and monitors.

For the next two days, I slept most of the time. Sometimes I was aware of Mama sitting by my bed, but most of the time I was trying to answer the nagging questions that were repeated over and over in my mind. "Why did I come back? How can I help others when my own life is in shambles?"

The auto accident had been my fault. I had blacked out behind the wheel of my car, a result of the stress I had been under since my estranged husband had run off with his girlfriend and taken our three-year-old son, Jimmy, with him. He had admitted an affair and asked for a divorce just as I was about to tell him I was expecting another baby. I had chosen not to tell him about the baby. He had promised to continue providing for me and our young boys. That promise was just one more deception. Taking Jimmy away from me was the final, most devastating blow.

On the third day after my near-death experience, I was lying in bed still hooked up to a number of things that made it impossible for me to move. I awoke momentarily to see a young girl dressed in bright red and white stripes come into my room. She was pushing a cart loaded down with fresh pitchers of ice water and orange juice. She set one of each on the table next to my bed, and left the room.

I closed my eyes again and drifted back to sleep. The next time I awoke the young girl was coming back into the room and one of the nurses was with her. I felt surprisingly better, almost refreshed.

"This patient can't take anything by mouth," the nurse was saying. "That's why you ran out of pitchers before your rounds were finished."

Then the nurse looked at the two pitchers the volunteer had left in my room. They were both empty. She strode over to my bed and examined the straps that confined me to the bed and my IV hook-ups. Everything was in place. There was no way I could have touched those pitchers.

"Maybe someone else came in and drank them," the candy-striper suggested.

"I was at the station the whole time," the nurse said slowly. "No one else came near this room."

After that, my recovery was rapid. The doctors were amazed and so was everyone else. Even more surprising to them was the fact that my brush with death had not adversely affected my unborn child. Bruises and contusions faded, all signs of internal injuries disappeared, and the leg that had been considered crushed beyond repair now required only a small ankle cast.

"It's a miracle," my mother told me the day they released me from the hospital. "I prayed for a miracle and God answered my prayer."

I wanted desperately to tell her that I had made my own bargain with God, but I was afraid to speak of my experience with anyone, even Mama. Four months later, I delivered a healthy baby boy. I called him David.

With no money to pay a private investigator, there was no further word on my husband or the little boy he had stolen from me. I was granted a divorce on the grounds of desertion. Life was difficult, but whenever I held David I felt a surge of hope. He was living proof of the miracles I had experienced. Perhaps his birth was also the beginning of the happiness I had been promised, a happiness that would only be complete when I had Jimmy back with me.

I was willing to do all that was expected of me. The problem was I wasn't sure exactly what I was supposed to do. The only thing I knew was that it had something to do with my psychic abilities. Since my journey to the other side of existence, they had become so strong, I was no longer able to deny them.

Joyce Martin is a nationally known psychic who has worked with police departments across the country helping to locate loved ones. Read her entire story in the book, My Bargain with God. *One high-profile case garnered a lot of publicity and led to a reunion with her lost son. Today Joyce resides in Tucson, Arizona.*

A Life-Saving Warning
By Ellie Ballentine

I was lying on my back, legs up in the air, in a teaching hospital in Brussels Belgium. We were living in a community called Woluwe St Pierre at the time and the hospital was about 15 minutes away. I was somewhere between exhausted and elated. I'd just given birth to our second son, Ryan. I looked over to see his gorgeous little body being bathed by his dad in a deep see-through plastic pail. One week overdue and he looked 2 months old and weighed in at just about 9 lbs 6 oz. I felt a sense of pure light and love.

At the same time, I was watching the student nurse who had been ordered to stitch me up. She looked pale and exhausted and I was concerned about how she was going to be able to perform the procedure assigned to her. As I continued to watch her closely, I remember a distinct moment where I felt a sudden shift in the way I felt. I had the thought "something just entered me." I was puzzled by this sudden thought. It didn't make sense. I began to panic a bit; I could feel my heart racing and the nausea was increasing by the second. I told the girl that I was suddenly feeling very sick. My body began to shake and I couldn't control it. The intern said that that was normal, that my body went through a shock and the shaking sometimes happens. To which the little voice in my head kept saying, "something is wrong."

At that point in my life my tendency was to not "rock the boat," and "they know better than me". I looked at my newborn son and decided to focus on him. Since Ryan was one week overdue, my parents were visiting from Canada and had tickets to leave that day. I wanted them to see us all together before they left. I also focused on introducing this new little one to his older brother.

My parents' visit went well, but at the same time I was constantly hearing a voice in my head that said, "something is not well." I had never been "spoken to" like that before. I could literally hear it in my head. I thought perhaps my hormones were bonkers so I was a little edgy.

That night I noticed my milk was not coming in. Ryan was hungry for more than I could offer. As I tried to get someone to help me, I also noticed that there were not that many people on staff. It was Easter, and there were only a few people on the floor. I did not see my gynecologist for the 2 days I was there.

I remember truly trying to catch the eye of one of the nurses to get her to listen to what I was sensing was going on; that what I was feeling did not feel like exhaustion, but like illness. She looked at me and said (in French) "I was there. You did not take an epidural so of course you are exhausted. I guess you're not feeling too proud now. You've exhausted yourself so you are not producing much milk. I'll give you some formula." My eyes widened and my jaw dropped. I was not going to get any sympathy or attention.

My husband picked me up the next day and home we went. We were about 3 months into living in a new city and country. My husband was overwhelmed with dealing with a new office, expectations and a travel schedule that meant he left almost every Sunday. As a couple, we were having difficulty dealing with the changes. I knew I was going to be left alone with a newborn, my 4 year old son, and this body that was not feeling well.

Now as many of you who are mothers with more than one child know, bringing home the next child is a big thing. I was focused on our first boy's response to having a sibling and sharing the attention. I was really thrilled when I heard him say, "Where is my baby?" He immediately loved his new brother and showed only warmth, love and a desire to keep him safe. For this I was grateful.

I remember that afternoon, I was walking up a flight of stairs and I became aware of an intense weak feeling and the voice began to speak again. Just hearing "something is wrong" was bothersome. I lay down for a moment, and then my body began to shake. I went to the bathroom and looked at myself. My breasts were small and depleted, I was flushed in the face, and I suddenly felt like I was going to faint. I reached for the thermometer and took my temperature. Beep beep beep 105F. I took it again. 105F. "Tom, do we have another thermometer somewhere?" I took it again. 106F! At that moment I actually paused. The last thing I wanted to do was state "there is something wrong." I took a deep breath and went to talk to my husband. He was silent as we packed up to go back to the hospital.

When we arrived, there was literally no one there to receive us. By this point, my breathing became shallow. I could barely hang onto Ryan on my lap. Tom put me into a wheelchair and wheeled me around looking for help. We were finally received and admitted back into the hospital. It took a couple of hours before someone actually came to see me. We were notified that they were very short of staff being Easter Weekend. They informed Tom that they would have to run some tests. They sent him home with my eldest son but I would not let them take Ryan. It just didn't make sense to me.

For what seemed like hours, I was poked and prodded, x-rayed and ultrasound-ed. They could not find anything. My heart rate was very slow and it took all my energy to just breathe. Then suddenly a deep, intense pain began in my uterus. Within an hour I could no longer hold my urine. Then it was my bowels and the pain just kept increasing and traveling to different parts of my body. It was at this point that a memory came to mind.

When I was very young, I heard the story of my father's mother dying at childbirth from sepsis. I felt very sad that my father lost his mother and never knew her. Irrational I know, but I decided to take on this pain because I did not want to imagine my father feeling the pain. Then another thought came to mind. I had done the same thing with my husband. He too, lost his mother at a young age.

I realized that I was going to carry on this story in my family. "No way!" As soon as that was clear, I began to pray. "God, I know we've had chats before but I want a direct connection, NOW! I am very clear that I do not want to fulfill some family story of sons losing their mothers at a young age. I no longer want to take care of this story. I get it, I get it. I have to stop being responsible for their feelings, their sadness, conscious or unconscious. I don't have to fix them. I don't have to take care of them."

I remember looking at Ryan at this point. He was smiling and cooing. He took the bottle well, no complaints, then off to sleep. I was deeply aware of a kind of light surrounding him. I would try to keep the door closed, because once it was closed there was an energy in the room that I cannot describe. It was as if the room was no longer part of the hospital. I would keep my eye on Ryan then on the sky. I prayed and prayed for guidance.

I was writhing in pain most of the time. But I guess exhaustion took over because I managed to fall asleep. I only know this because of the dream I had. I dreamt that I was in total blackness and nothingness. Then I was aware that I did not have a body but I was part of a liquid. Suddenly, I was pushed through a tunnel and I saw other cells floating by, other forms in bright colors. I was moving quickly and trying to see everything as I sped along. Suddenly some of the shapes in this liquid turned into monsters; viper heads with fangs, monster heads jumping out at me. I was aware that I was part of my blood. Then, a final "whoosh" sound occurred and I was snapped into a wakeful state and that voice in my head shouted "IT'S A BLOOD INFECTION!"

I rolled out of bed grabbing the I.V. drip gizmo and ran down the hall yelling in French "C'est une infection de sang! C'est une infection de sang!" The nurse tried to calm me down and I immediately complied, but with a firm voice demanded a blood test for blood infections. I got one. Sure enough, streptococcus group A came out positive in the tests.

I was rushed to ICU where they made an insert into the main artery in my neck and began to flood me with antibiotics. The pain began to subside within a few hours. By the end of the day, my temperature came down and I could feel my body accepting the help. The voice in my head was gone.

I had always thought of myself as this individual body oriented mind. I am Ellie. I am here in this body looking out through this set of eyes. However, this "confrontation" in my life presented me with an opportunity to consider beyond what I would lose or of what I was afraid. I took away my body/mind as my reference point. Everything had changed. I surrendered to what I can only describe as an interior subjective force, or life itself. No matter what I was feeling, fear, pain, I aligned myself with that force.

I felt for the first time that I was not alone. That there was a greater power that did not come from my head or my heart, but came from deep inside me. The wisdom, the knowing, the creativity was a part of me, not external to me. That was one of my most precious discoveries in my evolution of being a human being.

Ellie Ballentine, MBA, MA psych is the Mindset Mentor for high-performing individuals who are ready to transform their setbacks into breakthroughs. As a licensed transformational therapist with real-world business experience, Ellie has a distinctive understanding of the real-life challenges that people face. She is an engaging facilitator and draws both on her personal knowledge as a former consultant and experience of traveling and living in Europe and North America. Throughout her career she has effectively helped clients overcome addiction problems, heal broken relationships, resolve career obstacles and get back to living life on their own terms. Visit her website: www.EllieBallentine.com.

The Voice
By Andrew J. Whelchel III

The sun had just come over the horizon. I'd finished my pre-flight inspection. Every detail had been checked, and double-checked for safety. The air was warming quickly and a breeze out of the West meant an uphill take off would be necessary. With my tail wheel instructor, Charlie, securely strapped in the back seat, I spun the prop bringing the Champ to life. It was my pride and joy, a plane painstakingly restored by my grandfather and me before his passing. It sat for many years before I'd taken an interest and made it once again airworthy.

Sitting at the end of the runway, Charlie and I agreed, off the ground by the trees halfway down the runway or shut it down and skip today's flight. Full throttle and we were rolling, as the trees passed the window the vibration stopped, the wheels were off the ground. But I distinctly, remember the sick feeling in the pit of my stomach telling me something was wrong.

The runway disappeared, but just as we crossed over the road we lost our lift. We were returning to the ground, unplanned. All the training took over, and survival became the priority. People often say this type of moment causes your life to flash before your eyes, but there was no time. I pulled hard on the stick, and pushed the rudder pedal so hard my foot went through the floorboard just as we slammed into the ground cartwheeling wingtip-over-wingtip, but it was far better than the nose in approach we were originally destined for.

Only semi-conscious I wrapped my arm under my leg and with one fierce tug I pulled my mangled appendage back into the cockpit. Charlie, ribs broken, and larynx bruised helped me out of the shattered hulk that barely resembled an airplane. I tried to insist I should walk home and dial 911. A woman, who I've still yet to meet, rode over the hill on her horse and dismounted to help hold me down. Thankfully it wasn't long until a paramedic I recognized arrived. Her familiarity allowed me to relax and pass out for the ambulance ride.

My body lay broken and twitching with shock on the emergency room table. I could feel the blood seeping from my body and watched as it stained the sheets. With my adrenaline pumping I lifted a nurse right off her feet demanding she, "wake me up from this dream," before being restrained.

The room grew cold, my peripheral vision blackened, and crept inward. The voices grew faint until they faded away.

I've always been very reluctant to discuss those few missing moments. But I will say it made understanding the warm white light people associate with these moments very personal. However, my most lasting impression will be of "The Voice." I truly believe that what was said was for me only, and to most other people it would make little to no sense. But it's something I felt as much as I heard.

Then, I sucked in a deep breath and opened my eyes to the paddles that were about to be used to resuscitate me.

"You won't need those," I told the doctor who look as shocked as I did, but without missing a beat laid them down and moved on to temporarily patching holes so I could be moved to surgery. With my new found purpose I was lucky to be back on my feet in only a few months. Oddly enough during this time I also lost my home to a flood, lost my car, and spent every penny I had to pay medical bills. I didn't care!

Nothing could take away the sweet smells, or every tasty bite of food. Living on bonus time was a gift. With my newfound purpose I've been able to accomplish more than I could have ever dreamed possible. Smiling far more often than frowning because I know my happiness comes from two simple things. Nothing here is as important as it seems, and shedding worry is empowering. Secondly, we all have a purpose, and according to many experts, you only need to listen and you will find yours.

Happiness Awaits You!

*Andrew J. Whelchel III has been president of National Writers Literary Agency (founded 1981) since 1997. The agency has become a part of Whelchel's larger Global Talent Representatives, Inc., a company with an eye for management detail and a focus on media capital. Whelchel has placed clients' with publishers such as Bantam/Dell, Simon & Schuster, Career Press, Random House, Waterbrook Press, McGraw-Hill, Black Heron Press, Putnam, Berkley, Kensington, Amadeus Press and a host of other publishers. This in addition to film deals with MGM, Singer-White Entertainment Warner Brothers, Cheyenne Entertainment (a Bruce Willis company), Michael Taylor (producer of Phenomenon), Orly Adelson Productions, HBO, Disney, CBS and others. Past, and present clients have included Emmy Winner Josh Kotzen from ABC Television's Good Morning America Weekend Edition, best-selling author C.J. Box (*Open Season, Savage Run, Winterkill*), and other works with internationally best-selling author Ian Halperin, international bestseller Doug Rushkoff, the American Society of Golf Course Architects, and legendary Warren Miller Films.*

What is Happiness Really?
By Jamie Clark

Happiness is defined as a state of well being and contentment. However, what makes each of us content is as varied as the many grains of sand found at the beach. We all want to find happiness and fulfillment in our lives. Sometimes we are so engrossed in our daily routines, that happiness and fulfillment seem just out of reach, so we go on surviving life, instead of living it.

For me, a Psychic Medium, the most extraordinary happiness is being able to make a difference in people's lives. It is a rewarding experience to be able to bridge the connection between people living here to those they have loved and lost, as well as having the ability to give both insight and guidance regarding the daily choices that ultimately make up our life's path.

Feeling lost when my family was taken from this life, I didn't know where to turn or what to do next. I began to look for a way to help myself heal. By searching within and focusing on developing my spiritual gifts, I was able to realize how to make my own connections with my loved ones. I became more determined to live a fulfilling life. The more I developed, the more complete my life became. I realized I wanted to share with others the gift I had given to my loved ones and myself. To be able to assist others with the healing process and the path to happiness, this would be my ultimate goal.

I use the analogy that we are all at one big party, and our loved ones are having a marvelous time, but we are the ones sitting in the corner with our heads hung low and our spirits down and out. Our people want to connect with us as much as we want to connect with them, and sometimes we do not know how to initiate this type of communication. I feel honored to be the bridge that initiates this reunion.

So many clients come to me with feelings of devastation over their loss, thinking that they will never speak to their loved ones again. Some come to see me as a last resort. There are also those who have never been to someone like me and are afraid. I put them at ease by letting them know there is absolutely nothing to be fearful about in communicating with your loved ones on the other side. Making these connections gives a solid validation that your loved ones are never far away.

A validation is founded on truth or fact. When a person makes a transition to the other side, they retain their same personality, characteristics and memories. During a session, information will be presented that will confirm the person's identity. You will receive details which will assist you in validating the continued existence of your loved ones. During your own connection, you may not notice these signs, as they are very subtle. They are excited to have the opportunity to affirm, through their personalities and communications, the signs that you may not be listening to. It is extremely healing for all involved.

Those I read for are introduced to a whole new reality. It's a mind-opening experience. A session can be very emotional and some may even cry. When that happens, I know I am doing my job in a very powerful way. By the end of the reading, I am already seeing a transformation and the beginnings of a smile. Most say that more than ever before, they feel alive and at peace. They begin to live again rather than survive, realizing that the capability exists to make their own connections.

The pain and loss of my family was impetuous in getting me to do this as a full time profession. In experiencing the power of love and compassion for those I read, I receive just as much healing for myself, as I give to others. By connecting with many, I know and realize that our family and friends are alive and still communicating with us. I am fortunate to do what I love and love what I do.

Life is an amazing journey, and it is nice to know our loved ones are still with us, here and now. I am on my way to a self-fulfilling prophecy. It is my pleasure to be able to assist as many others as I can along the way. Won't you join me? Happiness awaits you!

Jamie Clark is an internationally known Psychic Medium currently living in Phoenix, Arizona. He is 1 of 16 contestants chosen to compete on Lifetime TV's "America's Psychic Challenge." Today Jamie demonstrates his abilities to the public with group seminars, TV and radio, as well as, private and individual sessions. Web site: www.jamieclark.net Email: info@jamieclark.net

STEPPING STONES

Have you ever felt that a loved one who has crossed over is nearby? Have you received a message or a sign from a departed soul?

Do you know anyone who has had a brush with death? If so, how did it change them?

_____

_____

_____

_____

What is your perception of life after death?

_____

_____

_____

_____

List the gifts you have in this lifetime and how you can use them to attain happiness for
yourself and others.

_____

_____

_____

_____

Consider using meditation to communicate with loved ones who have crossed over.

One proven method is to pose a question to a person who has passed away before falling asleep. It often prompts them to appear in your dreams with an answer.

LaVergne, TN USA
06 April 2010
178332LV00003B/2/P